Inspire
Motivate
Collaborate
Leading with Emotional Intelligence

Bobby Moore

Foreword by Douglas B. Reeves

National Middle School Association
Westerville, Ohio

Betty Edwards, Executive Director
April Tibbles, Director of Publications
Carla Weiland, Publications Editor
John Lounsbury, Editor, Professional Publications
Edward Brazee, Consulting Editor, Professional Publications
Mary Mitchell, Designer, Editorial Assistant
Dawn Williams, Publications Manager
Lindsay Kronmiller, Cover and Layout Designer
Marcia Meade-Hurst, Senior Publications Representative
Peggy Rajala, Publications & Event Marketing Manager

Library of Congress Cataloging-in-Publication Data

Moore, Bobby, 1963-
 Inspire, motivate, collaborate : leading with emotional intelligence / Bobby Moore ; foreword by Douglas Reeves.
     p. cm.
Includes bibliographical references.
 ISBN 978-1-56090-229-4
1. School management and organization--Psychological aspects. 2. Educational leadership--Psychological aspects. 3. Emotional intelligence. I. Title.
 LB2805.M637 2009
 371.2001'9--dc22
                    2009020811

National Middle School Association
4151 Executive Parkway, Suite 300
Westerville, Ohio 43081
1-800-528-NMSA f: 614-895-4750
www.nmsa.org

About the Author

Dr. Bobby Moore, currently a middle school principal and educational consultant, conducts workshops, coaches educators, and presents at both national and

international conferences. In 2007, he was one of only four secondary principals in the state of Ohio originally selected by Governor Strickland to serve on the Governor's new Creativity and Innovation Institute to help generate ideas for reforming education in Ohio. Dr. Moore is principal of Canaan Middle School, which has received both state and national recognition for outstanding student achievement, value-added growth, and meeting the emotional and social needs of students. A former Ohio Assistant Principal of the Year, he has also been a teacher, varsity basketball coach, and athletic administrator. Dr. Moore has had articles published in several national and state publications. His professional interests and presentations focus on leadership, school reform, student learning, assessments for learning, professional learning communities, professional development, team building, organizational development, character education, and emotional intelligence. His personal interests include snow skiing (out of helicopters and in the backcountry), cycling, swimming, fishing, and other fitness activities. He lives in Plain City, Ohio, with his wife, Deborah Moore, Ph.D. Dr. Moore can be reached at www.inspiremychool.com

Acknowledgments

It is impossible to accomplish writing such a book as this without the support and encouragement of some very important people in my life. First, I would like to give a special thanks to my editor, Carla Weiland from National Middle School Association for her interest, passion, and professionalism throughout this project. I would also like to offer a sincere "thank you" to Carla Edlefson, Ph.D., of Ashland University, for without her, much of the writing and research for this book would have never been completed. She has modeled the highest levels of emotional intelligence while working with me as a mentor, advisor, colleague, and friend.

I would also like to acknowledge the staff of Canaan Middle School, Ashland University Doctoral Program, and National Middle School Association. I have never been associated with a more inspirational, dedicated, and child-centered staff than that of Canaan Middle School. Whether a teacher, cook, custodian, assistant, counselor, or aide, your passion to put kids first has always been recognized and is noted. Ashland University's Doctoral Program was an integral piece in my leadership and emotional intelligence development. I am appreciative to each of the faculty members and staff that helped me along the way. I would like to thank National Middle School Association for its mission of focusing on students in the middle, and helping develop better teachers and administrators along the way.

I would like to acknowledge that the assessments in this book would not have been possible without the work of Dr. Benjamin Palmer and Dr. Gilles Gignac of Genos. In addition some of the leaders, researchers, and coaches in the field of emotional intelligence such as Richard Boyatzis, John Reid, and Joseph Liberti have unselfishly shared their knowledge. I also would like to thank my professional colleagues who are my support systems and critical friends who have not only helped me in increasing my own leadership skills, but also have lent their professional support, friendship, and camaraderie: Doug Carpenter, Ed Eppley, Tom Burton, Phil Harris, Chris Piper, Neil Gupta, Pam Noeth, and Ron Widman.

Finally, I would be remiss if I did not mention the love, encouragement, and support that I received from my wife, Deborah Moore, Ph.D., throughout this as well as many other endeavors in my life.

Table of Contents

Foreword *Douglas B. Reeves*

While emotional intelligence is not a new concept, it remains more the subject of earnest advocacy than practical application. Leaders and leadership preparation programs make an eloquent case for emotional intelligence, but too frequently the daily stress and anxiety of leadership renders a serious focus on this essential skill a low priority. Getting the job done means, in this distorted view, that leaders can dominate their subordinates today, and deal with feelings tomorrow—or next week or next month, assuming that there are not similar crises in the future. In this immensely practical book, Dr. Moore makes the case that emotionally intelligent leadership is the priority, and that other priorities will never be accomplished without a consistent and thoughtful application of the components of these essential leadership practices.

If the case for emotional intelligence is so clear, why is the skill so rare? First, leaders underestimate the impact of their own emotions. Second, leaders excuse their emotionally toxic behaviors due to their own high levels of stress. Third, despite the proliferation of evidence and advocacy on behalf of emotional intelligence, the daily exigencies of leadership create a chasm between intention and reality.

Moore synthesizes a decade of evidence that concludes the emotions of leaders are contagious. A kind word eases the tension of the entire office, and a curt exchange places an entire organization into an emotionally driven flight-or-fight response. Nevertheless, too many leaders dismiss the value of their own positive and negative emotions. Even small gestures, such as thank-you notes, personal recognition of extra effort, and inquiries into family and personal interests can have an enormously positive impact on staff morale, particularly during times of stress and anxiety. Strangely, however, school leaders do not even know the names of all of their staff members in some institutions, and "recognition" is more likely to be noticing error than appreciating success. That is one reason that Moore's assessments are such an important part of this book. Not only are the questions designed to elicit deep personal reflection, but the format engages both leaders and staff members to consider the attributes of emotionally intelligent leadership. When these assessments are rigorously and consistently applied, a leader will have the feedback necessary to gain and sustain effective leadership practices. It is particularly noteworthy that these chapters link specific behaviors—not merely attitudes and beliefs—to emotional intelligence. Most people describe emotional intelligence by its opposite—the domineering, insensitive, and uncaring leader. But putting into practical terms the behaviors and skills associated with positive emotional intelligence traits is an entirely different matter. While every candidate for a leadership may claim to like people and understand the value of appreciation of colleagues, how many of your subordinates can provide an affirmative response to the question, "I have received praise in the past seven days?"

Even self-aware leaders who know the value of emotional intelligence sometimes ignore or abuse their subordinates, excusing their behavior as a result of their own level of stress. A toxic board member abuses the superintendent in public who then intemperately chides a principal in public who is then dismissive of a teacher who, in turn, finds it easier to justify an outburst directed toward a student. Even our pets resonate with our emotions, with the warm, enthusiastic, and unconditional greeting from the family dog quickly transformed into a sullen retreat when we return their love with our scowl. "I've had a bad day," becomes the catch-all excuse for behavior that, like the pebble in the pond, radiates outward to influence the environment all around us. Challenging this excuse, Moore suggests a series of detailed conversations, laden with feedback for leaders. When taken seriously, these conversations will prevent leaders from becoming infectious agents of stress. No amount of external provocation justifies failures in emotional intelligence. Indeed, the only way to stop the cycle of negative emotional contagion is for the leader to consistently gain feedback, recognize their behavioral patterns, and transform negative emotional energy into goodwill.

The third reason that leaders fail to apply the lessons of emotional intelligence in daily practice is the overwhelming burden of daily emergencies. The late bus, out-of-control student, absent teacher, angry parent, demanding boss, unrelenting regulatory environments, inquiring media, and a thousand other tasks too frequently elevate the urgent over the important. Moore wisely suggests that these sources of stress should not be ignored but rather must be reframed from fires that must be extinguished to valuable sources of information. As a practical matter, leaders cannot and should not evade their daily responsibilities, but they can monitor the impact that these demands have on their own emotions and the psychological conditions of their colleagues and students. The goal is not the stereotypical calm of the monastic retreat or the bewildered but clueless optimist. Emotional intelligence, Moore concludes, is a skill to be learned, honed, and practiced. There is a reason that experts in yoga call their discipline "practice." It is not a virtue that mysteriously descends upon the practitioner, but rather is a state that is pursued with discipline and consistency. Similarly, in the midst of even the most challenging day, emotionally intelligent leaders recognize that there are elements of "practice" in which they too can engage—attentive listening, personal appreciation, and confrontation of negativity, to name just a few. Just as leaders routinely set goals for achievement, discipline, attendance, extracurricular activities, and a host of other areas, so, too, must they set goals for emotionally intelligent behavior.

The good news of this book is that we know what to do. The more challenging news is that we do not arrive at our destination until the day we either stop leading others on our own terms or the day we are carried out of our office in a pine box. Reviewing the assessments in this book forces me to recognize how often I fall short of the mark, and I have had a series of successively more challenging leadership responsibilities for 35 years. Surely I needed Moore's advice when I was a 21-year-old commander in the military three and half decades ago, and I need it today as the leader of a complex international organization. I am certain that you, too, will find these wise words and challenging assessments of value.

Dr. Reeves is the founder of The Leadership and Learning Center. The author of more than twenty books on leadership and organizational effectiveness, he has twice been named to the Harvard University Distinguished Authors Series and was named the Brock International Laureate for his contributions to education.

A Note from the Author

This book was developed to support school administrators, teacher leaders, and teachers dealing with the emotions, conflicts, and challenges of creating a successful professional learning community. The book will also be an excellent resource for entry level principal and teacher education programs. Although the theory and practice of creating a professional learning community have been researched and well documented, the skills and strategies to deal with the emotions associated with the process have not received the attention they deserve. A professional learning community must be built on trust, hope, and respect. When a learning community focuses on the intellectual, emotional, and physical needs of its students, there will be times when colleagues will be forced to balance patience and persistence. After committing to each other and the cause, educators can inspire those around them to believe that all things can be accomplished. This inspiration, along with the ongoing process of building collaborative skills, can motivate everyone in the school. However, regardless of how attainable and worthy this goal is, the emotions associated with change and school reform are what limit our success.

Typically, when people discuss the nature of emotions, they quickly become overwhelmed. Emotions are in us and around us all the time, and in everything we do, both at school and at home. Sorting them and dealing with them can be an overwhelming challenge.

From my work with principals and teachers from rural, urban, and suburban districts, I have learned that many of the problems in creating student-centered schools are caused by the interactions of the adults, who are in good faith at work on this mission. However, as educators, our lack of training on team building, collaboration, dealing with change, and leadership creates roadblocks and barriers to success while draining valuable energy, motivation, and enthusiasm. If schools can become autonomous and provide educators with the necessary "non-teaching" skills and organizational capacities, as professionals we will be able to collaborate, celebrate, dialogue, debate, problem solve and hold each other accountable so that all children will learn and always be the main focus of our schools.

This new professional development for educators will challenge the adults in the buildings to question preconceived mental models and paradigms that limit them from becoming all that they can be. This collaborative effort will take individuals who not only can understand and express their own emotions, but also can understand the emotions of others. Schools will become not only places of learning for children and adults, but also places of encouragement, inspiration, and support as well.

Without question, the challenges of demographics, diversity, and economic disadvantages affect our children. But, as school leaders we can cultivate a culture of commitment; lead, collaborate with, and support our staffs as we learn to work together, appreciate each other; and tap into every one of our strengths and abilities. If we do this, I firmly believe we as educators can solve nearly every problem in our schools. Having the ability, knowledge and skill to work together as adults will help us find the courage to do so.

So, I invite you to use this resource to become a leader of high emotional intelligence who will leverage your strengths, refine your weaknesses, and learn some new skills to make a difference in your school.

Introduction:
Why Emotional Intelligence?

Of the many skills required for successful school leadership in the 21st century, none is more important than the ability to put together a team of committed and collaborative staff who hold a common vision. Developing and maintaining a cohesive team with a relentless focus on student learning is a daunting task. To cultivate a culture that is always challenging the status quo and where excellence is the expectation, school leaders will need to learn, develop, and demonstrate high levels of emotional intelligence. Michael Fullan (2001), a leading authority on educational leadership, indicates the success of 21st century school leaders will increasingly depend on establishing successful relationships, leading change, and dealing with emotions in turbulent times.

Effective leaders will need to transform schools into autonomous, professional learning communities that embrace change and create high-performing learning environments for students and teachers (Moore, 2007). Many educational researchers cite the importance of handling emotions for the leaders of such reforms (Fullan, 2001). Emotional Intelligence (EI) is an individual's ability to perceive emotion in self and others, understand it, and then manage it (Salovey & Mayer, 1990). A high level of emotional intelligence is an essential component of effective leadership (George, 2000). Studying emotional intelligence provides school leaders with the information and awareness necessary to guide staffs as they develop a common vision for their schools, maintain their focus on achievement for all students, and create a school culture of trust and respect. According to a study of Fortune 500 companies, EI was twice as important as cognitive ability in predicting outstanding employee performance and accounted for more than 85 percent of star performance in top leaders (Hay Group, 1999). And the good news is, emotional intelligence can be developed and improved!

The professional learning community and emotional intelligence

No recent reform initiative has led to more significant school improvement than the creation of professional learning communities (PLC). The two biggest obstacles in turning a school into a PLC have been 1) school leaders' focusing on terminology and perceptions rather than "practices" (Dufour, 2007), and 2) the inability of school leaders to deal effectively with emotions during the implementation process (Moore, 2007). While there have been a number of informative books about creating a PLC in schools (Blankenstein, 2004; Dufour, 2007), there has been little to support educators in recognizing, assessing, developing, or improving their levels of emotional intelligence.

Educators naturally feel somewhat anxious, even overwhelmed, when they initiate a major school reform. Sarason, as cited in Dufour & Eaker (1998), stated, "the turmoil associated with school reform cannot be avoided, and how well it is coped with separates the boys from the men and the girls from the women" (p. 49). While school leaders often experience anxiety and stress that lead to role strain (Bredeson, 1993), it is also normal for their teachers to experience anxiety and frustration during the stages of implementation. This is not a reflection of poor leadership, but a necessary and unavoidable reality. I cannot recall the number of conversations I have had during the last several years with administrators who have advised that a school leader cannot wait for 100 percent, 75 percent, or even less buy-in to initiate some of the changes crucial for school success. To a person, these leaders believed that had they waited for a very high level of buy-in before implementing change, anxiety and churning would still have occurred. Wheatley (1999) wrote in *Leadership and the New Science:*

> Once I understood the nature of the work, it helped me relax and be more generous. I learned that people get frightened if asked to change their worldview: And why wouldn't they? Of course people will get defensive; of course they might be intrigued by a new idea, but then turn away in fear. They are smart enough to realize how much they would have to change if they accepted that idea. (p.176)

Heifetz and Linsky (2002) believe successful leaders must learn to "address emotional as well as conceptual work" (p.116). Senge (1990) shared the view of one CEO who believed it was unfortunate that leaders pursued physical and intellectual development over emotional development, as emotional capacities may be more important in reaching one's fullest potential. In this book I hope to help you understand the major part that developing your emotional capacities has to play in reaching your fullest potential.

Sala (2001) reported that as soon as many businesses and organizations learned the value of emotional intelligence, many emotional intelligence programs emerged as part of leadership training and identification programs. Boyatzis said that these programs were designed to (a) educate people about emotional intelligence, (b) evaluate their strengths and weaknesses, and (c) develop and enhance their ability to display greater emotional intelligence (as cited in Sala, 2001).

Components of the program

This book provides a program that explains why improving your emotional intelligence will make you a better leader and how to go about it. The program includes a combination of case studies, my experiences as an emotional intelligence and school administrator coach, and emotional intelligence self-assessment and staff assessment instruments developed by Genos, an international company led by experienced researchers.

Many emotional intelligence assessments and coaching programs adopted by Fortune 500 companies and other business executives cost hundreds of dollars. Unfortunately, few schools are ever provided such resources for training, identifying, and developing their leaders. This resource, however, will help school leaders identify their strengths and provide opportunities for them to develop their emotional intelligence without having to spend thousands of dollars.

The book's case studies, both genuine and adapted, examine challenges that are often emotionally charged and that are faced by school leaders on a daily basis. The case studies allow you to gain valuable and wide-ranging experiences without having to be personally involved with the associated conflict. Through the case studies you will acquire insight into your own emotional intelligence as you learn from Rick, principal of a high-achieving school, who fails to get a position for which he felt ready and qualified; from Chip, assistant principal and athletic director, husband and father, as he encounters trust issues, challenges to his decisions, and stress from meshing multiple roles; and from Paula, a principal, as she strives to be persuasive but not aggressive and to treat superiors and staff alike. Analyses of these and other case studies combined with suggestions for improving your own emotional intelligence are all included here.

Assessment tools

The Genos Emotional Intelligence Inventory Self-Assessment and the Genos Staff Rater Emotional Intelligence Assessment—provided in the appendix are important items. While the self-assessment is a good place for you to start improving your leadership skills, the staff assessment will provide valuable information about how others perceive you as you deal with emotions, make decisions, and inspire and influence the school culture. Several popular books have relied exclusively on self-assessment tools.

However, research indicates the congruency of self-assessment and staff assessment scores is the best indicator of leaders' effectiveness. Managerial Self-Awareness (MSA), the relationship between a leader's self-perception and others' perceptions of that leader, has been researched in a variety of studies (Bass & Yammarino, 1991; Church, 1997; Fletcher & Baldry, 2000). Because many leadership studies show MSA is one of the most important skills for those tasked with inspiring, leading, and supervising employees, we include the Staff Rater Assessment. To skillfully lead professional learning communities, principals must understand how others in the school perceive them and their actions.

The results of your assessment along with the reflection activities and goal worksheets will help you identify emotional intelligence dimensions that are your strengths and the emotional intelligence competencies most critical for your current job. Based on all this, you will be guided in creating a development plan with specific strategies for improving your emotional intelligence.

The improvement process

After compiling the results from your assessment, creating your development plan, and reading and completing exercises in the book, you will immediately begin to practice new behaviors at work, but this will not be easy. Developing new behaviors and skills takes hours of repeated practice. You will need to constantly focus on your commitment to developing skills and behaviors that will make you more effective as a school leader. There will be times when you sense success in using your new skills. Because writing about your successes reinforces the behavior, it is important to record those successes in the log included in Chapter 5. There will also be times when you revert to your former behavior patterns, especially in times of crisis. Record these incidents as well, and during reflection, write about alternative actions you could have taken to achieve a more desirable outcome.

Recording and reflecting upon your experiences will be a final, ongoing step in improving your emotional intelligence.

Reflection: Key piece of the puzzle

People with high emotional intelligence are not usually high in every dimension or competency of emotional intelligence, nor are they perfect in behaving appropriately. However, people high in emotional intelligence understand the importance of regularly reflecting upon their emotions, decisions, and interactions with others. Some even share their reflections with trusted colleagues or seek feedback while replaying their interactions with others.

In my experience of coaching of school leaders, I have learned the enormous benefit of building time for reflection into the schedule. In follow-up interviews about the coaching program, school leaders indicated that reflection was instrumental in developing emotional intelligence, and that it was one of the best parts of the program:

> Self-reflection has been very useful to me. Self-reflection is something I don't normally take the time to do.

> I think the [coaching] sessions are very thought provoking. They really cause me to think of things I never thought of and in ways I have never thought. Reflection is the most valuable tool in the program.

> reflect and think about how you respond to people and emotions. I think we all make mistakes. We sometimes say "I won't do it this way next time," but the time comes and we do it the exact same way. ... Practice your skills and do some thinking in the down time, you can avoid those bad mistakes.

> One of the most beneficial parts of the process has been the journaling and reflection piece.

Find and schedule time for reflection in your personal journey toward improved emotional intelligence and become a far more effective leader.

Getting started

A brief history of the study of emotional intelligence will give you the needed perspective on this professional development opportunity. After reading the chapter, you will be directed to do your self-assessment. At that time, you may also ask your staff to assess your emotional intelligence. Chapters 2–7 will explore several dimensions of the Genos Emotional Intelligence Model and how they relate to school administration, as well as provide strategies for your development. Chapter 8 will share emotions and experiences of other school leaders during coaching sessions. Chapter 9 will provide examples of other administrators' goals and reveal their successful strategies. Chapter 10 will motivate and inspire you as former participants in an emotional intelligence coaching program share the transformations each has made since learning the importance of emotional intelligence.

My job as coach is not to give you all the answers, but to provide you opportunities to explore alternatives that would best fit your desired outcome. Your job is to select those strategies and tools that will best help you avoid succumbing to emotional hijacking and most support you in appropriately managing emotional situations. The books' charts and graphs will help you summarize your learning and assist you in creating a Personalized Development Plan for monitoring your future learning.

Good luck; now let's get started!

Chapter 1
A Historical Perspective

The nature of relationships among the adults within a school has a greater influence on the character and quality of that school and on student achievement than anything else. —Roland S. Barth

Daniel Goleman introduced the general public to the concept of emotional intelligence (EI) with his book *Emotional Intelligence: Why It Can Matter More Than IQ* (1995). When Goleman, a social science journalist for the *New York Times,* was writing his book, he discovered the work on emotional intelligence done by Salovey and Mayer (1990). Although the term *emotional intelligence* appeared in Goleman's book title, his description displayed little resemblance to the model hypothesized by Salovey and Mayer. The book became a best seller, bringing the concept of emotional intelligence international attention.

Soon after Goleman's book was published, numerous claims about the value of emotional intelligence emerged. Skeptical about its validity, some scientists attempted to disprove the potential of emotional intelligence as a predictor. The controversy is, in many respects, similar to the one that surrounded multiple intelligences. Because they think intelligence and personality measures alone can predict performance and leadership effectiveness, and that emotional intelligence may be either one of them in disguise or a combination of the two, some scientists do not regard emotional intelligence as a new concept. While some scientists continue to argue about whether emotional intelligence is truly a type of intelligence or just part of a person's personality traits, many of them continue to assert that the research adequately supports the position that emotional intelligence can predict life satisfaction, effective leadership, happiness, and other desired qualities.

Models of emotional intelligence

Several models and measurements of emotional intelligence emerged and confused scientists and others interested in emotional intelligence (Palmer, 2003a). Bar-On (1979) and Goleman (1995) developed two of the earlier popular models, which have been used in a variety of settings. Sometimes these models are referred to as "mixed models" or "Trait EI"; they include

- Skills and abilities (emotional self-awareness, accurate self-assessment, self-confidence, empathy, organizational awareness, inspirational leadership, influence, developing others, change catalyst, conflict management, building bonds, teamwork, and collaboration).

- Personality traits (openness, conscientiousness, extraversion, agreeableness, neuroticism).

- Moods that have been identified and measured by other instruments. (Mayer et al., 2000).

Salovey's and Mayer's (1990) model has been defined as "Ability EI." Ability emotional intelligence can be measured through actual performance tests with correct and incorrect answers. Regardless of the researcher or emotional intelligence model, emotional intelligence is generally defined as the ability to effectively deal with emotions (Geher & Renstrom, 2004).

The Genos Model. Dr. Ben Palmer of Melbourne, Australia, surmised that some emotional intelligence instruments measured too many personality factors, while other instruments lacked any measurement of factors contributing to successful leadership (2003a). His research led to the development of the Swinburne University Emotional Intelligence Test, which eventually was renamed Genos. The Genos Emotional Intelligence Assessment is a reliable, valid instrument and meets the criteria established by the Consortium for Research on Emotional Intelligence in Organizations for its listing as a measure of emotional intelligence. Designed to be a workplace measure of emotional intelligence, the Genos instrument assesses the most definitive, common elements of emotional intelligence. The structure of this book is directly linked to the seven dimensions of emotional intelligence shown in Figure 1 that Genos measures.

Chapters 2 through 7 make up the heart of this book. Chapter 2 is devoted to emotional self-awareness, the foundation of emotional intelligence. Chapter 3 discusses the second dimension, the ability to successfully express emotions. By learning to effectively express their emotions, school leaders gain the capacity to develop cultures in which staff members can openly discuss feelings in an appropriate manner. Chapter 4 deals with one of the most important skills needed to lead change—emotional awareness of others. Leaders capable of discerning the pulse and temperature of their schools can improve their decision-making skills. Chapter 5 discusses emotions as a source of information. Emotional Reasoning, may sound like a paradox. While school reformers have emphasized data-driven decision making as necessary for leading school change, they have rarely included emotional information that influences the communication of critical decisions and the achievement of desired outcomes. Chapter 6 combines two very similar dimensions, emotional self-management and emotional self-control. Chapter 7 discusses the emotional management of others and helps you tap into the moods and emotions of your staff, which leads to increasing their commitment and performance.

Figure 1 The Genos model of EI comprises seven specific EI dimensions. The table below presents a definition of each dimension and outcomes that can be achieved from displaying each dimension effectively at work.

EI Dimension	Definition	Workplace Outcomes
Emotional Self-Awareness	The skill of perceiving and understanding one's own emotions.	• The capacity to identify and understand the impact one's own feelings is having on thoughts, decisions, behavior, and performance at work. • Greater Self-Awareness
Emotional Expression	The skill of expressing one's own emotions effectively.	• Creating greater understanding amongst colleagues about yourself. • Creating trust and perceptions of genuinesness amongst colleagues
Emotional Awareness of Others	The skill of perceiving and understanding others' emotions.	• Greater understanding of others, how to engage, respond, motivate, and connect with them • Interpersonal effectiveness
Emotional Reasoning	The skill of utilizing emotional information in decision making.	• Enhanced decision making where more information is considered in the process • Greater buy-in from others into decisions that are made
Emotional Self-Management	The skill of effectively managing one's own emotions.	• Improved job satisfaction and engagement • Improved ability to cope with high work demands • Greater interpersonal effectiveness • Enhanced productivity and performance
Emotional Management of Others	The skill of influencing the mood and emotions of others.	• The capacity to generate greater productivity and performance from others • The capacity to generate a positive and satisfying work environment for others. • The capacity to effectively deal with workplace conflict
Emotional Self-Control	The skill of effectively controlling strong emotional experience and associated behaviors.	• Emotional well-being • The capacity to think clearly in stressful situations • The capacity to deal effectively with situations that cause strong emotions

Emotional intelligence research

A number of studies have demonstrated the existence of emotional intelligence as an independent construct. Chubb and Moe, (1990), Evans (1996), Fullan (2001), and Schlechty (1997) have discussed the need for systemic change and school reform including the better education of school leaders. While there has been a growing acknowledgement among educators that emotional intelligence research is needed (Cherniss, 1998; Fullan, 2001; Williams, 2008), there have been few studies involving emotional intelligence and school leadership.

Emotional intelligence as predictor of leadership effectiveness.

Derksen, Kramer, and Katzko (2002) concluded that emotional intelligence measures something different than traditional intelligence tests measure. Higgs and Aitken (2003) concluded emotional intelligence may be as effective as leadership assessment centers in predicting leadership potential. Sy, Tram, and O'Hara's (2006) research confirmed emotional intelligence can have a higher predictive power of achievement, occupational success, healthy lifestyles, and relationship success than the Big Five Personality Factors. Law, Song, and Wong, (2004) also concluded emotional intelligence could be used to study leadership effectiveness. After reviewing more than 69 emotional intelligence studies, Van Rooy and Viswesvaran (2004) concluded emotional intelligence could be considered a valid, sound predictor of job performance.

Emotional intelligence and transformational leadership.

Transformational leaders influence, inspire, stimulate intellectually, and help their employees to grow (Burns, 1979). Mandell and Pherwani (2003) found a significant relationship between emotional intelligence and transformational leadership style. Barling et al. (2000) concluded that staff members viewed those individuals with higher emotional intelligence as displaying more leadership behaviors than individuals who had lower emotional intelligence. Gardner and Stough (2002) found that transformational leaders scoring high on emotional intelligence assessments exhibited more transformational behaviors than those who scored lower.

Emotional intelligence competencies of outstanding urban principals.

Williams (2008) studied the leadership characteristics of urban principals identified as outstanding. Peers and central office and union leaders identified

12 outstanding and eight typical principals, who supplied data through interviews, open-ended questions, and a variety of assessments. Williams discovered 13 emotional intelligence competencies significantly differentiating outstanding principals from typical principals. The competencies were (a) self-confidence, (b) self-control, (c) consciousness, (d) achievement orientation, (e) initiative, (f) organizational awareness, (g) developing others, (h) influence, (i) analytical thinking, (j) leadership, (k) teamwork or collaboration influence, (l) change catalyst, and (m) conflict management.

Effect of principals' emotional intelligence on student achievement.

Sala (2002) investigated the relationship of student performance, organizational climate, and the emotional intelligence competencies of 92 college principals (university personnel) in the United Kingdom and discovered students' academic performance was not significantly related to the principals' emotional intelligence. However, the institutions with higher student retention rates had principals who displayed more emotional self-awareness and social awareness. The study also revealed that a principal's social skills of empathy, organizational awareness, service, inspirational leadership, influence, developing others, change catalyst, conflict management, building bonds, teamwork, and collaboration are the most important factors in predicting the organizational climate of a school. The discovery that the principal's emotional intelligence may not directly affect student performance is similar to other findings in educational research that indicate the little direct effect that principals may have on student outcomes (Hallinger & Heck, 1996, 1998). However, emotional intelligence likely influences culture, climate, and other factors known to lead to increased student achievement.

Emotional intelligence and school leadership. In one of the largest studies on emotional intelligence and school leadership, Stone, Parker, and Wood (2005) studied 464 principals or vice-principals (187 men and 277 women) from nine different public school boards in Ontario, Canada. Researchers discovered principals and vice principals in the above-average leadership group scored higher than the below-average leadership group on total emotional intelligence in an assessment measuring four broad dimensions (intrapersonal, interpersonal, adaptability, and stress management). The above-average leadership group also scored higher than the below-average leadership group in behavior- and task-

oriented skills of empathy and interpersonal relationships, but not of social responsibility. Concluding by advocating that professional development include programs on empathy, emotional self awareness, and flexibility, the authors proposed using emotional intelligence assessment in recruiting school leaders.

Effect of emotional intelligence coaching on school leaders. My own research, Moore (2007), used a case study approach to investigate the emotional intelligence of three school leaders and their reactions to emotional intelligence coaching. Using the Genos EI Assessment Tool, which gathered data from the leaders themselves, as well as from their superiors, peers, and direct reports, I assessed the three school leaders before and after four months of coaching. Data included transcriptions of the coaching sessions plus individual and group interviews. The data revealed that school leaders grew in emotional intelligence, believed emotional intelligence was one of the most important skills for school leaders, and benefited from the coaching.

Summary

Having been the subject of research for little more than a decade, emotional intelligence is still in its infancy stage; and researchers and psychologists continue to discuss the validity of the proposed theories. Emotional intelligence, just like the theory of multiple intelligences, may never be universally accepted. But just as educators continue to use strategies based on the theory of multiple intelligences, educators may use emotional intelligence models to develop leaders capable of meeting the challenges of the future.

Steps to improve your emotional intelligence

1. Before beginning Chapter 2 take the EI (Emotional Intelligence) Self-assessment in Appendix A (p. 99) and score it as directed in the Appendix.
2. Administer the Genos Staff Rater EI Assessment in Appendix B (p. 103). Having both a self- and a staff assessment gives a more accurate, detailed picture of your perceived emotional intelligence than the self-assessment alone. Alternately, you can do the self-assessment now, and after finishing the book and feeling more confident about your goals and understanding of emotional intelligence, you can administer the staff assessment. Feel free to choose either method—there is no right or wrong approach. Whenever you

do use the staff assessment, to reassure your staff of the confidentiality of their responses, ask a trusted colleague to collect the assessments.

After receiving your staff assessments, you will score them using Appendix C (p. 105). After taking your assessment and scoring your staff's assessments, you will be given a total emotional intelligence score. More important than your review of the overall score will be analyzing how you scored in each dimension shown in the chart in Figure 1 (p. 9); your results will help you identify your strengths and possible areas for improvement.

Regardless of a person's title, the person receiving feedback from an assessment usually reacts defensively if scores are low in any category or dimension. I think of this as the grieving process because, although great leaders are aware that they are not perfect, many are surprised by the feedback and feel the loss of their former perception. In spite of your disappointment in the feedback, consider this an opportunity for development.

The Genos assessment score is not intended to determine whether or not you are a successful leader. The fact that you are interested in developing your EI skills speaks to your leadership skills. Effective leaders rarely score high in all dimensions or have strengths in every dimension.

3. Complete Appendix D (p. 107), "Examining the Gaps Between Self and Staff Scores" to further help you define your most needed areas of improvement.

➡ Questions for reflection

After reviewing your scores from your self and staff assessments and the comparison of them in Appendix D (p. 107), answer the following questions.

1. In Appendix D (p. 107) review the correlation of the emotional intelligence dimensions to the survey questions.
2. Which scores were higher for each question– your self-assessment score or the average of the staff assessment scores? If the scores are different, why do you think there is a difference in perceptions?
3. In what dimensions did you score the highest? The lowest?
4. Based on both your self and staff assessments, what strengths can you continue to leverage?

5. Identify two dimensions that are your lowest according to the survey questions. What outcomes could you expect at school if you were to improve in these areas?

6. To begin your journey you must visualize the type of emotionally intelligent principal you would like to be by completing the following questions.

    A. Describe the behaviors of a school leader who would have scored high in the dimension of Emotional Self-Awareness.

    B. Describe the behaviors of a school leader who would have scored high in the dimension of Emotional Expression.

    C. Describe the behaviors of a school leader who would have scored high in the dimension of Emotional Awareness of Others.

    D. Describe the behaviors of a school leader who would have scored high in the dimension of Emotional Reasoning.

    E. Describe the behaviors of a school leader who would have scored high in the dimension of Emotional Self-Management.

    F. Describe the behaviors of a school leader who would have scored high in the dimension of Emotional Management of Others.

    G. Describe the behaviors of a school leader who would have scored high in the dimension of Emotional Self-Control.

    H. What dimension was your strength and what area could you improve the most?

    I. If you were to improve in several of these dimensions, what improvements would you notice in (a) relationships, (b) stress, and (c) quality of life?

Chapter 2
Emotional Self-Awareness

Understanding and perceiving your own
emotions is perhaps the most important
dimension of emotional intelligence.

In this chapter we will discuss the origins, range, and importance of emotions as well as how to identify them. Most important, we will begin our discussions on how you can gain control over your emotions and learn to use them for increasing your productivity, relationships, and satisfaction with life.

Origins of emotions

Much more than just our feelings, emotions are sources of valuable information (Palmer, 2003.) Emotions may seem to suddenly "appear," but they are actually products of thoughts and experiences. Refusing to acknowledge emotions and lacking the ability to explore them present many problems for school leaders. Conversely, leaders who recognize emotions and can predict their sources will be prepared to deal with the challenges in leading a school.

One of the best explanations of how emotions work comes from a story first told by Dr. Joseph LeDoux, a New York University professor who was one of the pioneers in studying emotions. Most of us know how we would respond to seeing a rattlesnake as we were leisurely working in our garden. Startled and scared, we would feel our heart rate jump and our breathing increase rapidly. We would be experiencing a "fight or flight" response or an "emotional hijacking." During an emotional hijacking we may not be at our best in communicating, thinking, or responding because the amygdala, the part of the brain that controls emotion, would have triggered the emotions of fight or flight. The fight or flight response is an evolutionary adaptation that helps species survive predation; as soon as an animal is perceives danger, all its bodily systems are on high alert to battle the predator or escape it. Totally focused on survival, the amygdala, the part of the brain dealing with emotions, sacrifices accuracy for speed. Thus, the amygdala has a tough time differentiating a real threat from a perceived threat. Both a rattlesnake and a stick that looks like a rattlesnake stimulate the amygdala and trigger the same fight or flight response. Our brains, as with other animals, are hardwired to produce all-out, overreactions when we encounter a rattlesnake, or a stick looking like a rattlesnake. Sometimes this works against us school leaders as we sort through the overabundance of messages on our computers and try to ascertain who has legitimate questions, who is making a sarcastic complaint about a decision we made, and who seems to be raising a serious problem but just needs us to listen.

The amygdala cannot distinguish rattlesnakes (real threats) from the hundreds of perceived threats a school leader faces regularly in the workplace. These perceived threats are often referred to as triggers. Triggers and our emotional reactions to them limit our success and cause most of the challenges we face in our administrative careers. Principals have identified such triggers as an upset parent on the phone, a staff member resisting change, and a call from the superintendent. When one of these triggers sets off the amygdala, our emotional reaction can resemble that of our picking up a rattlesnake.

Origins of perceived threats. Many of our perceived threats arise from childhood experiences, illogical thought patterns, or misperceptions that trigger our emotions. Can you recall an unpleasant childhood experience that still evokes a strong emotion today? Now, as an adult, when you are confronted with a similar event, do you experience a similar emotion? Thought patterns and misconceptions based on past experiences have shaped our present-day mental models and paradigms and can be limiting factors to our success. The mental models themselves cannot limit success; it is our emotional reactions associated with them that determine our ability to lead. And whether a threat confronting us is real or perceived, our emotional reactions significantly impact our interactions with parents, students, and staff members. Have you ever reacted poorly to a staff member's question in a staff meeting? Was the staff member's question a real threat or a perceived threat?

During coaching sessions, many principals have shared that they have felt attacked and very uncomfortable in staff meetings. Old mental models of the need to defend themselves from attack set off their fight or flight responses which then resulted in overreactions to the pressure. Even though these principals could cite numerous examples of legitimate questions and positive staff members, it is the negative experiences of the past that really control present-day behavior of the principals. To counter this, principals practiced challenging their mental models and reassured themselves that any teacher asking a question has a positive intention and is not mounting an attack. The few seconds it takes to think this through delays the amygdala from inappropriately providing the emergency response (the defensive overreaction), and the principals could maintain composure.

Understanding and perceiving your own emotions is perhaps the most important dimension of emotional intelligence. In addition to maintaining your composure and gaining respect in times of crisis, you model the importance of treating everyone with respect.

The importance of identifying emotions

The following case studies demonstrate the importance of leaders' being able to identify their feelings. Not doing so prevents one from building bridges with teachers, parents, and community stakeholders and from having vital information needed to make good decisions; and it creates unhealthy, stressful situations. As you read the case studies that follow, see if there is any behavior to which you can relate.

Impacts relationships with parents. For ten years, John has been a principal of a high-performing school in an influential suburban district. Parents call him weekly to ask about a detention, a grade on a test, playing time in a team sport, or some other event that is "a matter of life or death" to the parent but only trivial to John.

Although John understands the difficulty parents have in remaining objective when their child is involved, he usually becomes very frustrated by the amount of time he needs to spend talking to parents about such issues. During his early years as principal, his frustration led to anger and at times caused him to react negatively to parents. But John now thinks of himself as an emotionally intelligent principal. When John notices his pulse or respiration increasing, his hands getting sweaty, or that knot in his stomach, he stops and separates his thoughts from his feelings. He knows to ask himself, "What am I thinking, and what am I feeling?" John also identifies what actions may have evoked his emotion and then reflects on whether in the long run sharing this emotion will help or hurt him in carrying out his responsibilities. John has learned how critical his awareness of his emotions is to his leadership success.

Impacts decision making. A school leader who participated in a study of school leaders and emotional intelligence coaching, Rick shared during an early coaching session:

> There are times when I clearly feel like I am not making the best decision based on the emotional status of a situation even though I try to. Lots of people say it takes 24 hours. I believe it takes me 48 hours.

From coaching Rick learned that before making decisions or reacting in times of uncertainty or conflict, to search his feelings, analyze viable options that would produce his desired outcome, and then take action. Rick proved that as difficult as it is to change behaviors, with practice and committed effort, it can be done.

Early in his coaching program, Rick had shared a story illustrating how his illogical thoughts tended to cause him to become angry. After he observed one of his new, aspiring teachers teach a great lesson, Rick completed a positive evaluation with a few suggestions for improvement. Although teachers have an opportunity to write comments on the evaluation, most teachers usually just thank him and sign the form. But in this particular situation, the teacher did not.

> She asked if she could take the observation and read it, and I said, "Sure." I almost took it as, "Does she not trust me?" This is something I really need to work on. I don't know how you get past this assuming you know what teachers are thinking or what their motives are. I assumed the reason that she wanted to read this further is because she really doesn't trust the administration and that I might have put something bad in there.

Although no teacher had ever disagreed with an evaluation he had given, when the teacher wanted to take the evaluation home, he jumped to the conclusion "Something must be wrong," which led to his anger. When we separate our thoughts from our feelings, we can usually identify the reason for our emotions, and we are primed to make better decisions. Rick later learned he could have separated his feelings and thoughts and asked himself for any positive reasons why the person might have wanted to read over the evaluation. The strategy of assuming positive intentions can often prevent an emotional hijacking.

Impacts reactions to others. Paula, a principal in the Emotional Intelligence and School Leader Study, shared how valuable it was for her to recognize her emotions during a situation in which she became frustrated with one of her supervisors' insensitive comments.

> This really upset me. But I did not react. Although I was very upset inside, I knew it was not productive to say anything. My thoughts were that she does not realize what she said. She did not mean to offend me. I actually thought about this in my head. Typically I would have responded to something like this. This time I chose not to even bring it up.

Every day, all day long, there are constant miscommunications in the workplace. As you begin feeling a negative reaction to another person's comments, consider that the person may not be communicating as effectively as he or she might like, or that you might be perceiving a nonexistent threat based on a past experience. Paula believes emotional intelligence coaching and identifying her emotions have improved her reactions to others, and she spends a lot more time reflecting on how she handles school situations than she did in the past.

Builds bridges to stakeholders. The challenge of being emotionally intelligent is the unpredictability of crises and conflicts. However, when principals learn to quickly recognize their emotions and predict why they might be feeling as they do, they can calmly remain open-minded, bring reasoning and perspective into play, and choose to respond as emotionally intelligent leaders. One school leader, unaware of his rising anger, allowed his posture and tone of voice to upset a parent.

> I was at a booster meeting, and a parent had requested from a previous meeting to see our vendor's contract with the school district. She was not happy that the athletic boosters had to buy their products from this vendor, even though this vendor had committed several hundred thousands of dollars to the school district's new athletic facilities. When reviewing the contract, the booster member noticed that the school district would receive complimentary products each year to use at the district's discretion. The booster member wanted to know who got the free products. I answered that we use the free products during professional development meetings throughout the year. The parent was very upset. This really hit a nerve. My body tone and voice both showed I was angry. I did not handle it well; I was emotional. I should have watched my tone. The booster member was very quiet the rest of the meeting.

When asked to explain his options for handling the situation, the principal explained, "I should have just handled my emotions and not gotten angry." I coach my clients to realize that they are not their emotions, and I advise them not to think in phrases such as, "I am mad," and "I got angry." You may feel mad or angry, but you are so much more than your emotions; they are an element of you. Rather than "handling your emotions," school leaders need to identify their emotions, identify the cause of the emotions, and choose a productive strategy for managing them.

After a coaching session the above school leader understood that he had now created a situation in which this person might not bring him bad news or legitimate questions or concerns unless he rebuilt their relationship bridge. To be a great leader, you need people around you to bring you all the news and their concerns, no matter how bad. And there isn't enough time in our days to spend it rebuilding relationships after every emotion we experience.

How to identify your emotions

Now that you know how important it is to identify your emotions, how do you go about it? The most important part of the process sounds very simple, but it requires much discipline: take the time to explore why you are feeling what you are feeling—stop, look, and listen. Emotion is sometimes thought of as E(nergy in) MOTION; self-reflection at that point may seem like the hardest thing in the world to do, but it becomes easier with practice. When you feel an emotion, identify why the feeling is there. Why do you feel sad, angry, or happy? If you decide the emotions is anger, then ask yourself, "Why anger? Did someone intentionally cause this, is there a real threat, or has the amygdala sacrificed accuracy for speed yet again?"

If the threat is real, you will need to manage your emotions and choose an effective strategy for de-escalating the situation. As the leader of an emotionally intelligent culture, you cannot afford to inappropriately react to people upset with you, and you can use the opportunity to model the behavior you want your school to exhibit.

Strategies for slowing down the urge to lash out and giving yourself time to choose wisely could include taking deep breaths, counting to ten, asking to continue the conversation at a later time, or communicating that you have hurt feelings. And even if the other person has initiated the confrontation, you must take responsibility for renewing contact with the person and "clearing the air."

More than once in my career, when I have explained in a calm, rational manner how a colleague has hurt my feelings by making some comment, the colleague has shared that he or she was feeling angry and upset about something else entirely and has apologized. Nearly every time this has happened, a productive, healing dialogue has followed. In contrast, early in my career as a principal, before studying emotional intelligence, I spent a vast amount of time repairing relationships that I had broken with my sharp tongue.

Questions for reflection

1. Think about a time during a school day when you overreacted to someone's comments. Might your overreaction have been caused by something that had happened earlier in the day and that was totally unrelated to this particular conversation? What were you feeling at the time of the first incident? What were you thinking at the time of the second incident?

2. Typically, when you get upset or angry about something, how long does it take you to calm yourself? Do you always realize you are angry or upset?

3. Do you recall ever making an important decision while you were emotionally hijacked? Did it turn out to be a good or bad decision?

4. Are there certain times of the day you experience more stress or frustrations than others? If so, what do you usually do when you become aware you are stressed and frustrated?

Steps to improve your emotional self-awareness

1. Take time during the day or week to explore your feelings and thoughts. Try to differentiate between the two. Increase your vocabulary related to emotions by writing words that best describe your feelings (not thoughts).

2. When an event occurs that creates stress or conflict for you, explore the strength of your emotions during the event. Identify the fundamental emotion that was evoked in you. How strong was the emotion? What behavior resulted from the emotion? Was the behavior impulsive? Can you connect it to your past in any way? Were you able to stop, look, and listen? Did you use another strategy to "buy yourself some time" to avert the fight or flight response?

3. With a trusted colleague, share what your feelings were during the day of the event in Question 2 above. Differentiate between feelings and thoughts during your discussion.

Chapter 3
Emotional Expression

I used to think I handled my emotions well; I would set them aside. Did what I did anyway, not because of how I felt, but despite the way I felt. There was no room for emotions in the workplace. —School Leader

This chapter discusses the importance of principals learning to appropriately express their emotions, the spectrum of emotional behaviors, coaching strategies for helping you express your feelings, and suggestions for times when it is NOT appropriate to express your feelings.

The importance of sharing emotions

In Buckingham's (1999) groundbreaking work *First Break All the Rules: What Great Managers Do Differently*, the author identified 12 key questions to which an organization's staff must be able to answer "yes" to qualify as having a culture of excellence.

1. Do I know what is expected of me at work?
2. Do I have the materials I need to do my work?
3. Do I have the opportunity to do what I do best every day?
4. In the last seven days have I received praise?
5. Does my principal or someone at work care about me?
6. Does someone at work encourage my professional development?
7. Do my opinions matter?
8. Does my school's mission make my job feel important?
9. Are my coworkers committed?
10. Do I have a best friend at work?
11. In the last six months has someone talked to me about my progress or given me feedback?
12. Do I have opportunities to learn and grow or for advancement? (p. 28)

Note nearly half the questions (numbers 4, 5, 6, 7, and 11) Buckingham identified as paramount to a productive culture can be tied to an emotionally intelligent leader who is comfortable sharing emotions.

Praise shows caring. An emotionally intelligent principal recognizes and praises the work of students and staff members. The quick jump in going from good to great that our school made has been well-documented. Despite one of the lowest per-pupil expenditures in the state, we rank among the best in student achievement and value-added qualities. Trying to find our "magic formula" for success, schools from all over the state visit our campus. Although many best practices and a relentless focus on student learning are readily apparent, many school personnel see something else. Visitors comment, "We knew your school was high on collaboration and in using data, but we were surprised by the evident real caring about one another that is present." Cultivating such a culture starts with the principal. A principal's sharing love for the school and the happiness and pride the students bring him or her is a great model for the rest of the community. Although many school leaders avoid expressing emotions, I view such expression as my strength, and my staff is always aware of my emotions. I believe this has been an essential element to the many achievements of our school.

Positive outcomes of sharing emotions

Sharing emotions helps a principal be a leader and builds trust and respect in the school community.

Effective leadership. Your emotional stability establishes the tone for the school; things may not be stable at their homes, but at your school, students and staff need to be able to predict what will happen when bad things and good things occur. Both the staff and student body can learn that when they come to school, they are coming to an emotionally safe place.

Our school, like other schools, treats bullying as a serious issue, and the first line of defense against it is creating and communicating a positive vision of a school without bullying. Two years ago, a group of six to eight popular girls were always in the middle of any bullying or arguing at our school. After meeting with the girls, I went to every class and reinforced our procedures for preventing bullying and re-communicated a vision of a bully-free school in which students respect each other and are safe from put downs, teasing, and criticism. I told each class how I felt when a parent called, concerned about her child being bullied at school. I explained that no matter how disappointed, embarrassed, or angry I had felt, the parent's anguish about the hurt her child suffered was much, much deeper. I asked students to put themselves in the shoes of their classmates and openly explore and discuss what it would feel like to be bullied. As a leader, one must not only be emotionally intelligent, but emotionally literate, meaning you can openly discuss and talk about emotions and encourage others to do so. In your vision of your school at its best, are you the model for emotionally intelligent, emotionally literate behavior?

Establishes leadership. At your school, once you have shared your emotions of excitement about achieving goals or disappointment over not having achieved them, the achievement or lack thereof is then "official." One of the most significant findings of behavioral change research to surface recently is the importance of establishing and recognizing emotions. Years ago Dale Carnegie stated that people are not creatures of logic, but creatures of emotions. Years of hospital-related research reveals that regardless of the disease diagnosed and behavior modification necessary to add longevity, many patients return to old habits, even if it means a shorter life. But when doctors talk to patients about changing behaviors to allow for experiencing the birth of their first grandchild, playing with their grandchildren, or giving their daughters away in marriage, the positive emotions associated with the change are more successful. Nutritionists and dietitians have learned most people's success with diet plans is not based on the logic of maintaining a balance between calories consumed and burned, but the emotions based on looking and feeling thinner and on surviving to experience more of life. And rather than using logic to drive and lead change, some schools are tapping in to the emotions and hopes of a school community in which all teachers can collaborate and feel safe. Identifying, communicating, and using emotions are necessary tools to cultivate the culture you want. When I visit a school wanting to drastically change its culture to increase student learning, I often show a clip of the 1961 movie *Spartacus* starring Kirk Douglas and Tony Curtis after this brief introduction:

> Born into slavery during the Roman Empire and gladiator era, Spartacus learned to fight and was given food, clothing, and a "good" life (for a slave) at a gladiator camp. In the movie The Gladiator, Spartacus (Kirk Douglas) leads a revolution in which gladiators escape their camp and go village to village

releasing more slaves. Their goal is to reach the coast, gain the help of pirates, and sail to freedom in a new land. As they journey on, Spartacus and his troops continue to triumph in battles with trained Roman armies. At the movie's end, after pirates betray Spartacus and his troops, several Roman troops surround Spartacus and the few gladiators still surviving the days of fighting. The Roman commander, in an effort to identify Spartacus from the remaining slaves or slain bodies, offers the slaves a chance to escape death and return to the life of slavery by identifying Spartacus. Otherwise, all the slaves would be crucified along the road back to Rome. As Spartacus begins to stand to identify himself, every slave, one by one, stands and says, "I am Spartacus."

The movie clip is inspirational and really models an emotionally intelligent workplace. At first, caught up in the bravery and loyalty displayed to Spartacus, many people think the clip is modeling a high level of commitment to a leader. But the clip is about something much more complex than commitment to a leader. For it was not the fear of starvation, crucifixion, slavery, or death that enabled Spartacus and his troops to win so many battles against the Roman Empire or make their last stand on the hillside, it was the hope of freedom and a better life. We have known for years that fear is not a productive motivator over time. However, fear is the emotion that most leaders tap into when leading reform or change, intentional or not. Leaders, however, could tap into emotions associated with hope and what our school could be like if …

Following the film clip, we do a Hopes and Fears Activity. On large poster board participants write one to three fears, ones that will be barriers to the changes that they want to take place or ones that prevent them from making necessary changes. Then, reading aloud many of the fears, I acknowledge that they are real. I also remind them that courage is not the absence of fear, but the ability to overcome their fears. I encourage the principals to use a whole professional development session to explore each fear and not to dismiss or play down any fear. Next I ask the participants to write the hopes for their school if everyone involved could make the necessary changes to fulfill the hope. Just like in the Spartacus clip, it will be the hopes for a better place that will be the intrinsic motivator for change. By posting the hopes and referring to them often, you will reinforce the vision with staff members.

Builds trust and respect. Rick, the school leader you met in the introduction, was not chosen as principal of a new building, much to his surprise and dismay. On the "fast track" to becoming a principal at the age of 29, Rick had always been recognized as an outstanding teacher and leader. When the superintendent told him he needed to improve his leadership skills to become a strong candidate for future promotions, he felt overlooked and undervalued. A few weeks later, Rick decided to take an emotional intelligence assessment and participate in emotional intelligence coaching. One of his goals was to hide his youth and lack of worldly experience by personifying an image of toughness and strength rather than empathy or caring. During his professional training as a young principal, he had learned principals were more effective if they had a backbone and did not display emotions. "And empathy was the worst of all emotions." As Rick's coach, I explained although there are times when you need to be tough, displaying empathy and an understanding of others may be the most important characteristic of a leader. These could easily be the qualities that the superintendent referred to as missing from his leadership skills. By learning and practicing such skills, he might experience less frustration, better relationships, and more success.

Another video clip that I use features Ronald Regan addressing the nation following the space shuttle Challenger disaster. This clip mesmerizes the audience, and most every person remembers exactly what he or she was doing when Challenger exploded. The first purpose of this clip is to show an example of Reagan, "The Great Communicator," connecting and displaying empathy to the nation, and the second is to show how powerful emotions are. The reason people can usually remember what they were doing and where they were is that the accident evoked very strong emotions. I discuss with teachers that although many of the changes they experienced during their career were not as devastating as the Challenger tragedy, every change or reform initiative in their career probably evoked strong emotions that even now cause them to recall the time of change. Once you understand the depth and power of emotions, you can empathize with what your staff must go through to adopt new practices. When principals initiate reforms, teachers usually have to abandon some habit, practice, or belief to which they have been deeply attached. The change is loss, and principals need not only to recognize this loss, but to acknowledge it as well.

Barriers to expressing emotions

One of the biggest barriers to expressing emotions is understanding that it is okay to emote. People will recognize and appreciate the strengths of a leader who has the ability to express his or her emotions in a productive manner and does not overreact, causing rifts in relationships that later take time and energy to rebuild.

Expressing negative emotions. Although it can be a challenge at first, a principal must master the skill of sharing negative emotions in an emotionally intelligent way. Last year our superintendent had each building principal administer a tool that assessed the job stress level of each of our teachers. Many of the questions asked teachers to rate the level of stress they were feeling on a scale of 1–10, with 10 being the highest level of stress. The survey also asked for suggestions for alleviating some of the stressors. The majority of my teachers rated their stress levels low to moderate (lower than I expected). However, I was disappointed, even frustrated, by some anonymous comments and suggestions made about alleviating stress. In our next teacher's meeting I told teachers that I was very appreciative of the honesty and sincerity of the responses on the survey. I mentioned my pride in lower stress scores than I had expected and connected the low scores to the supportive culture they have worked so hard to cultivate.

Then I spoke about some of the suggestions and comments that disappointed me. While acknowledging that no one intentionally had disappointed me, I told them I was frustrated with suggestions such as higher teacher salaries, more reimbursement of college tuition, less focus on student achievement, and eliminating state achievement tests because I have not seen research showing them as viable stress reducers for teachers. I told them that the superintendent sincerely wanted suggestions for creating excellent schools without lots of teacher stress, and I considered some of their comments unnecessary venting that could have been more appropriately done at another time in our safe school environment. A few teachers were upset that I chose to question their responses; I remained firm in my position that they had not offered answers for reducing stress. Two diametrically opposing viewpoints were respected and heard because the stage had been set by my focusing on expressing my disappointment without being disappointed and my frustration without being frustrated.

When you are excited and happy, share your emotions and show your emotions. When the emotions are anger, resentment, or frustration, communicate your emotions without showing them. This allows other people the space and safety to share what they are thinking and feeling, and both parties reach a better understanding. A key to successful administration, it gains the respect of your school community.

Sharing emotions: Hard work—not for sissies. Another barrier to expressing emotions is the myth that showing emotions equates to softness. One common mistake is confusing soft skills with a "soft" person or an emotionally intelligent leader as a "soft" person. Having good listening skills, being attentive to people's emotions, and effectively expressing your own emotions do not make people "soft." When I improved my emotional expression, my leadership improved; and I am perceived by others as stronger than before. For example, at numerous times during meetings at various schools, principals have become inappropriately emotional or aggressive. I have learned that when I feel myself becoming overly emotional, I can soon de-escalate the situation. I have learned to identify and appropriately communicate my emotions and not to be trapped by them. You can be emotionally intelligent and have a backbone.

Coaching tips for expressing emotions

As you practice expressing your emotions, it is important to be sincere and not manipulative. I once worked for a leader who sent a letter to his staff once every year. Although I believed his letter was sincere, because this was the only time he ever took the time to share his emotions, the staff viewed the letter as a form of manipulation, rather than a sincere reaching out to them. Be careful not to use emotions to control, manipulate, or gain an advantage over people but rather to connect with them for mutual benefit.

Separate thoughts and feelings. One principal showed very high emotional intelligence in recognizing that sharing disappointment instead of anger would nurture his school community and poise members for future improvement. Sharing anger can give you a quick release of frustration; but in the long run, it makes others quick to blame each other so that someone else can be in the path of the consequences of your anger.

Jim, a middle school principal, is very driven and has very high expectations for his staff and students. For three years in a row, their building has received an excellent rating by the state department of education. Jim eagerly anticipated seeing student achievement scores and could hardly wait the three months for the release of the results. When the test results finally came to the school, Jim was very disappointed. Because the scores were lower than in the past, the school would lose its excellent rating. Disappointed and angry, Jim's first thoughts were, "Why did the staff and kids let me down?" But quickly separating his thoughts from his feelings, Jim realized that the students and staff would be just as disappointed as he.

In this case study, Jim's thoughts that the students and staff had let him down led to his feelings of sadness and anger. Recognizing that his thoughts were driving his emotions, he paused. He then replaced his first thought with the thought that his students and staff would be greatly disappointed; he let this second thought drive his behavior of displaying empathy and concern. Jim addressed the staff and told them that he recognized how hard everyone had worked to continue the outstanding history of success they had achieved over the last few years. He then informed the staff that this year's results were not as good and that the school would lose its excellent rating. The staff could easily see that Jim was not angry, but truly disappointed for the staff and teachers, as well as for himself. Jim expressed his feelings of sadness and disappointment at seeing the test results. He expressed his concern for how the public might respond, but more specifically his concern about informing the student body that the test goals had not been met. By openly sharing his emotions in an appropriate manner, Jim connected with his staff more on this day than he had the three years prior when the school had met their state test goals. Jim had learned how to effectively express his emotions.

Write notes of appreciation. Writing notes to staff, students, and parents thanking them for their efforts when something goes well is a good practice; don't ever take for granted that they automatically know you appreciate them. In addition to writing notes, principals must also encourage and provide resources for teachers to write notes to one another. One year we gave all of our teachers dippers, buckets, and note cards shaped as water drops. It was our goal to frequently fill each others' buckets with positive notes, praise, or feedback. If someone witnessed someone sharing negative comments, we would politely ask him or her not to dip water out of our buckets. We also have custom-printed praise cards that make it simple for staff members to write notes to one another. When a staff member gets letters from the principal and peers frequently during the year, there is a culture of caring, support, and encouragement.

For more than a decade, I have been fortunate to work for a superintendent who has cultivated a family atmosphere in our district by making time for teachers, visiting school buildings, and frequently writing letters and e-mails of sincere appreciation. Here is one example of the many communications he has sent.

JA Family Members,

Well, it's that time of year. It's time for snow shovels and scrapers. Time to deal with the cold and blustery Ohio weather. Time for fireplaces and snuggling up with loved ones. And time for me to take a minute to thank each of you for all you do for our kids.

It's been a while since I sent out a big "thank you" to everyone … and for that I apologize. It is so easy to get caught up in the daily tasks that consume each of us. When that happens, we often forget to tell others that we value their work, that we are thankful for all they do, and that they are valued family members. I send you my deepest gratitude for your efforts in helping make our system better every day. **I am so proud of our school district … and it's because so many people here have big hearts and never lose focus on our central mission—OUR KIDS!**

Whether you drive a bus, cook a meal, calm an angry parent on the phone, give extra time to a kid who needs extra help or support, help create a building block for our success, or perform one of the many other daily tasks around here, **what you do and how much you give to others matters.** It's what sets our district apart from so many others.

Each day I marvel as I hear about or see things happening around the district. There are so many examples of "high touch," caring people here from one end of the district to another. I regularly receive and read surveys from parents new to our district, people who base their perceptions on others who live in the school district, family members, or friends. Time after time their comments are consistent with what we get from our three-year surveys with comments like:

"People here care."

"Based on what I've heard, I wouldn't want my child to go anywhere else."

"It seems so warm and friendly here, almost like a family."

"People here expect a lot, but give a lot to make sure students succeed."

"There seems to be a sense of pride among those who work for the school district that both my kids and my family want to catch."

And the list goes on an on. People do notice what you do, how much you give, that we try to work together as a family, and that what we're doing for kids is meaningful. **None of this would be possible without the efforts and commitment of many people, including you!**

Today, I was at a meeting out of the district and I was approached by not one, not two, but three different people asking about our school district. Questions like:

- "I hear people love your district. What are you doing out there?"
- "I bump into people all the time that are trying to send their kids to your school district. What's the magic formula you're using that is making parents feel your district is where they want their kids to be?"
- "How are you able to achieve such exceptionally high student performance?"

We're doing terrific work here … and we're always working to make things better for kids. That is not possible without the time, effort and commitment of many. Your efforts do make a difference here.

I thank you for all you do and pledge to continue to work side by side with you in our ongoing effort to make the Jonathan Schools a place we can all continue to be proud of.

Doug C.

Interestingly, Doug Carpenter, Ph.D., superintendent of more than 23 years in our district, never signs his letters with his title or degree, just "Doug." His skills in emotional intelligence have served the district well during his tenure as superintendent.

Watch body language. Research of common experience makes it clear that facial expressions and body language communicate emotions. One of the most impressive presentations I have ever seen was in Malaga, Spain, by Dr. Harold True, who had made hundreds of films of facial expressions each lasting nanoseconds. During his presentation he morphed different expressions using the various pieces of film of the eyes, mouth, and different parts of the face. I realized how powerful our body language (particularly facial expressions) is in communicating accurately or sending mixed messages about our emotions. Although they could see only parts of a face, people were amazingly accurate in reading emotions. We have all heard that crossing your arms when someone is talking can send the message that you are not open to what the other person is suggesting. It is important to be aware that your countenance, body position, and physical habits all are sending messages about what you are feeling, regardless of your words.

Conflict resolution through e-mail. Another coaching tip for emotional expression is to avoid expressing negative emotions through e-mail. This was an area in which Rick needed to improve his leadership effectiveness: expressing his emotions when he was upset or dealing with conflict. Needing time to process his emotions before responding to conflicts led him to respond to events via e-mail. Although a necessary tool, e-mail can create substantial problems if overused, especially for resolving conflicts. Rick wanted to improve his ability to deal with people face-to-face during times of conflict.

> I feel like I am pretty good in writing. Because of my booming voice and facial expressions, teachers often seem scared to death when I approach them face-to-face. I articulate better in writing than I can in my spoken words.

It also gave Rick more time to respond to a situation. Although taking his time in responding was a great strategy for dealing with emotions, he could check for understanding and demonstrate more empathy face-to-face .. Although Rick thought he was leveraging his strengths by writing his feelings in e-mails, his inability to control the reader's perception through body language and tone during the exchange, rather than resolving them, sometimes escalated situations.

Share both the good and bad. The principal should share enthusiasm over reaching goals as well as learn how to share concern about consequences of not making goals. Remember, when it comes from you, it's official. As a leader, you can shape the community's processing of events. You can positively motivate students and staff to achieve more than they ever thought possible.

Tom was a new principal who rarely expressed his emotions. In spite of his organizational skills, instructional leadership skills, and management skills, he struggled to communicate with his staff. As part of his emotional intelligence development, he made a point of expressing in his opening day presentation that he understood and shared in his staff's excitement about and pride in achieving an "Excellent" rating. As he spoke, he smiled, stood tall, and clapped during the conversation about the rating. He went on to express his disappointment about the failure of the operating levy at the polls. At a coaching session, he shared the noticeable improvement in connection he felt with the staff; he told of several staff members noting a difference in him that day. As leaders, we often confuse strong and stable with not showing or expressing emotions. A principal's strength and stability is not threatened by the expression of his or her emotions. In fact, people regard leadership skills as more impressive if they include the ability to express feelings appropriately.

Being fair. Nothing can jeopardize a leader's influence more than perceptions of having favorites or not being impartial. But the truth is every leader will have "favorites," or staff with whom the principal is closest. Rather than ignoring it, acknowledge these people as your support system and communicate to your staff that these relationships will not impact the fairness and equity of treatment of staff. Following my first year as principal, my teachers completed a staff rater instrument similar to the one included in Appendix B. The instrument provided feedback to me about how I was perceived as an instructional leader, manager, supporter, and coach; it rated my organizational skills and visibility, and my ability to maintain direction and set a vision. One of my lowest ratings was on favoritism. When I reviewed the results of the assessment with the staff, rather than becoming angry or defensive about the staff's perception that I had favorites, I acknowledged that I do have favorites. I pointed out that I did allow every staff member who needed to leave early or come in late to do so, that I had covered classes for almost every teacher, and that all their budgets were nearly the same. I explained my belief that there is a difference between equity and fairness and levels of relationships. I explained my tendency to talk and spend more time with teachers who, like me, were willing to openly share emotions as we talked. I pointed out that I seemed to converse with people who did not always agreed with me, but who liked to debate, dialogue, and examine educational issues. I shared my goal of addressing this perception and building high quality relationships with all my staff members. Amazingly enough, addressing this concern and openly inviting deeper levels of conversation including the sharing of emotions has improved all our staff relationships.

Remember, courage is not the absence of fear, but triumph over fear. I was not afraid to address a concern or a negative perception. And during the conversation, staff members came to view me as not just their principal, but as a fellow human being, who, like them, is capable of having different levels of relationships with different people, without jeopardizing equity and fairness.

When not to share emotions

Although people want to be led by leaders who have feelings, principals should explore their emotions and decide what impact sharing their emotions will have on the school culture during an event or situation. There will certainly be times when it is not appropriate to share your emotions. A principal can make this determination by reflecting on the outcome sharing an emotion will have on their staff, students, or parents. The issue is not that expressing too many emotions can have a detrimental effect on your leadership as much as the importance of your demonstrating stability.

Once I worked with an administrator who often used his emotions to manipulate the staff. Whenever there was a situation in which he felt the staff perceived him as ineffective, he would play the emotion card. Sharing family issues or challenges, he sought empathy from the staff. Although the strategy worked for a year or two, the staff eventually began to feel manipulated and trust issues arose.

As mentioned earlier, you can express your emotions without being overly emotional. I recall watching a principal address his staff about a situation in which he felt a lack of support. He reminded his staff that during his 20-year tenure, he had supported and encouraged them to take risks outside their comfort zones. Although the principal was angry and very disappointed about the events that had occurred, he never let his emotions get the best of him. He communicated his disappointment and his previous anger; he did not display it. Mirroring the principal's stability and calmness and listening attentively, the staff appreciated the principal sharing his feelings and committed to doing a better job of supporting him in the future.

➤ Questions for reflection

1. Would your staff describe you as a person that effectively and appropriately expresses your emotions? Why or why not?

2. Think about a time recently that you have expressed your emotions to a staff member. Were the emotions positive or negative? Are you better at expressing positive or negative emotions? Are you better at expressing your emotions to certain staff members, or are you able to express your emotions in front of the entire staff?

3. Have you ever considered a school leader "weak" for expressing emotions? Why or why not?

➤ Steps to improve your emotional expression

1. Take the time each day to express an emotion to a trusted colleague.

2. Write a sincere thank you note in which you communicate a feeling.

3. Ask a colleague after a meeting or event in which you spoke or made a presentation whether you effectively expressed any emotions.

4. Reflect on how you may have used your tone of voice, facial expression, or body language during a meeting or event. Get feedback from a trusted colleague.

Chapter 4
Understanding Others' Emotions

> I totally changed my perception about what other people feel. I never considered it before. It's not that I did not care; I thought it was irrelevant. —Chip, Assistant Principal

People do not quit their jobs; they quit their bosses, according to an old maxim. It follows then, that in education the 50 percent of teachers who leave the field within their first five years are leaving their principals, not education. While I am not ready to accept this assumption, I do believe that a principal's level of support, encouragement, and mentoring during a teacher's initial experiences is critical. If principals were more aware of and sensitive to teachers' emotions, they would offer more encouragement and support. And for the many principals leading their schools through change, the ability to perceive and understand the emotions of others may be the most valuable skill of all.

Emotional intelligence empowers school leaders

Understanding others' emotions provides you with valuable leadership information. When you understand the emotions people are experiencing and, when you don't understand them, if you take the time to explore the thoughts and reasons behind the emotions, your awareness of the realities of your school community will increase. With this information you will "have your hand on the pulse" and know when it is time to be persistent and when it is time to be patient.

Cultivating a culture of commitment. If you accept the challenge of understanding what your staff is feeling, then you can cultivate what I call a "culture of commitment." This culture will enable you to successfully manage resistance and directly deal with noncompliance, which is essential if you, your staff, and your students are to achieve the school's mission. Just as important, when you display an understanding of your staff's emotions, your staff will reciprocate and work hard at understanding your emotions as well. Not only does it strengthen everyone's feeling of community, the quality of work that takes place in such a school is amazing.

After reading much of Richard Dufour's work, I have avoided using the word "build" or "develop" when discussing or coaching about culture. Cultures are like gardens and not like buildings (Dufour & Burnette, 2002). Gardens need watering, weeding, fertilizing, and are in need of constant need of care as compared to buildings that may need periodic maintenance. In fact, most homeowners and architects would be annoyed or frustrated to build a structure that needed the same attention as a garden. But cultures built on trust, respect, and high commitment to excellence are more like gardens than anything else. The failure to accurately portray the necessary work to "maintain the garden" in preparing leaders has led to much of the frustration they face when trying to build rather than cultivate their school cultures.

While I was in the final stages of writing and editing this book, I had a ski accident serious enough to make me miss nearly a week of school. The timing of the accident was horrible: near the end of Christmas break and just a few days before the end of the semester. However, the event just reinforced how lucky I am to work with our staff. In our school our students have electives that change every semester, and it is my responsibility to schedule these courses. Usually the week before the semester ends, there is a lot of re-organizing and re-shuffling due to students' changing electives, students' enrolling late, or even students' choosing to stay in their current elective another semester. As this scheduling hassle hung over my head, I was already stressed by doctor appointments, physical therapy, and not being physically able to complete a full day of work. Having committed to getting the scheduling done on time, when I came into school, I found that a teacher had met with the students involved and had updated the new semester list for all electives. On her own time! I was so elated. More than a demonstration of that teacher's leadership, it was a demonstration of empathy as well. I could not remember when I was touched so much by a teacher's act of kindness. I delivered to her a note thanking her for her thoughtfulness and her leadership. She said that she had wanted to use some of the additional personal planning time in her schedule to do something for the school. Because these types of behaviors and actions often happen in our building, our school is an example of a culture of commitment that enables us to achieve much success.

Addressing noncompliance. Failing to address staff members not in compliance with the school mission or school processes is a huge mistake for school leaders. Although school leaders may rationalize that their inactions on this problem are "keeping the peace" or not "rocking the boat," they are doing just the opposite. By failing to acknowledge staff members' not honoring commitments and not following through on tasks important to student and school success, the principal is sowing toxic weeds instead of removing them from the garden. Do not confuse patience with procrastinating or refusing to deal with noncompliance. This is detrimental to the overall success of the school and displays fear rather than courage.

Confusing noncompliance with resistance. Another mistake that principals low in emotional intelligence make is confusing noncompliance with resistance. Resistance is more closely related to the ultimate goal of commitment than people realize and is not noncompliance, which is actual nonconformance to requirements. I try to learn from the questions that resisters ask; their questions help me know how to refine my communication of the goal as well as force me to think about every aspect and impact of a decision. Leaders should embrace resistance. To revisit our gardening analogy, when staff members ask questions about the fertilizer, the need for watering, why they are growing certain plants, or even imply they are not excited about horticulture, the principal cannot confuse this with noncompliance. Even in the face of resistance, you have to believe in your teachers' professionalism, and that each staff member will till and nurture the garden. When principals confuse resistance with noncompliance, they create barriers to performance and drain staff members' motivation.

During my first year as a principal in a newly configured middle school with new teachers from three different buildings, I made this mistake. From day one, our school attempted to be cutting edge. Voting not to follow the teacher association's contract, our school created larger classes for advanced students and smaller classes for struggling students. During the first year the teachers also gave up their thirty minutes of uninterrupted lunch so that I could trade a few aide positions for an additional teacher. Not all teachers agreed with this, nor did they all have a positive attitude about it, but everyone was compliant and fulfilled their jobs as professionals. I remember we were exploring new territory our first year and challenging nearly every paradigm of how schools are traditionally organized to create a new and successful school. Many times the teachers asked legitimate questions or expressed legitimate fears about our journey. Unfortunately for them, I was just starting my emotional intelligence development, and I was not as skilled as I am today in understanding others' emotions. Sometimes thinking of their very important questions and fears as "just poor attitude," I failed to acknowledge and value their behavior of fulfilling everything we did to the best of their ability. That first year was much more difficult than it needed to be for the adults in the building, but our newly designed school created instant and never-before-achieved success for our students. I apologize to my staff for my lack of understanding of their emotions during their first year of reform. On the positive side we have all discussed how much we have grown professionally and personally after our first year.

Focus on behaviors rather than attitudes. An example of focusing on attitudes rather than behaviors is provided by some of my interactions with Mrs. Williams, one of the most outstanding, patient, caring, and veteran teachers in our building. However, Mrs. Williams and I have a few very strong philosophical differences. Because I am a strong proponent of frequent assessments of learning, we have common assessments and short cycle assessments in every subject area. Not to be used for students' grades, these assessments provide information about what our students have not yet mastered nor learned so our teachers can reteach, intervene, or provide other high quality, corrective instruction. Before I completed my emotional intelligence training, I was often very frustrated that Mrs. Williams' attitudes towards these assessments were different than my views. I was afraid she would influence the staff to view these assessments as unnecessary. Although she did an outstanding job of assessments for learning, intervention lessons, and high quality corrective instruction, she did not believe in the new assessment processes I had initiated and thought they were just a trend in an era of student accountability. As an ultimate professional and one of the district's best teachers, Mrs. Willliams was 100 percent compliant with our school's process. But, my focus on attitudes rather than behaviors caused problems in our relationship, and others took notice. Instead of using her as an outstanding role model (compliant to the school's mission and vision, even though she was not in total agreement), I created a situation where people walked on eggshells around us, and some of the younger teachers may have been thinking, "If I do not agree 100 percent with Dr. Moore, regardless of how much I follow through, our relationship may not be as strong as others." What a mistake I was making! And thank goodness for my emotional intelligence training. The truth is I do not agree 100 percent with everything that the superintendent wants me to do, but I am compliant. You see, a culture of commitment is not just about being committed to duties, it is more than that. It is being committed to one another. It is naïve to think we can create a culture in which everyone is 100 percent committed to everything we do. However, we can create a culture in which 100 percent of the people are committed to each other. Once people are committed to each other, some are compliant to initiatives or tasks out of respect to their peers; some, because they agree it is the right thing to do; some, because it fits a vision of professional behavior; and some are compliant because they feel they have to be. The more you focus and acknowledge the positive behaviors in your school, more you will increase the positive attitudes and the higher level of commitment you will have. I have seen this transformation occur in several buildings. Today, Mrs. Williams and I have one of the best relationships in the school, and I trust her as much as anyone. My personal development has enabled me to appreciate all the gifts that she brings to our school. We still disagree on assessments and the era of accountability but are committed to each other.

Effectively lead school reform. Teachers inevitably will experience stress, anxiety, doubt, confusion, anger, and even resentment during the implementation stage of any new idea or strategy that inherently implies that what they are currently doing is "not good enough" or that "they can do better." While school leaders can choose their words carefully as they explain the reasons behind new initiatives or school reforms, leaders need to be sensitive to and aware of their staffs' emotions, which are real and justified. As hard as it is to change behaviors and actions on one's own, it is even more challenging when someone imposes those changes.

As mentioned earlier, people actually go through a grieving process when asked to change or stop doing something to which they are accustomed. Someone once said that all human beings have two basic fears; 1) the fear that they will not be loved, and 2) the fear that they may not be good enough. This makes sense and can be applied to the challenges of school reform. Whenever you ask teachers to change behaviors or teaching strategies, recognize that a reaction some faculty will have is that of inadequacy—whatever their current approach, it isn't good enough.

If this is combined with a lack of trust or respect—perhaps when principals are new to the position—then the fear of not being "loved" surfaces. When principals recognize these two most common fears and show empathy, patience, care, and respect during any reform initiative, their schools will more successfully weather the change process.

Strategies for understanding others' emotions

Collaborating on norms, exercising patience, developing timelines, controlling the emotional temperature, setting realistic expectations, and allowing your staff to experience their emotions are powerful strategies that emotionally intelligent leaders use.

Establish collaborative norms. Collaborative norms are rules or commitments people make to each other about how they will communicate, respond to conflict, and treat each other. Developing these norms is an important step in creating an emotionally intelligent school. After developing these norms, post them in the teachers' meeting area (or lounge) and identify one or two norms to practice in each staff meeting. In our school we selected these seven norms:

1. Pausing,
2. Paraphrasing,
3. Probing,
4. Putting ideas on the table,
5. Paying attention to self and others,
6. Presuming positive intentions,
7. Pursuing a balance between advocacy and inquiry

(adapted from the original work of Garmston & Wellman, (2009), *The Adaptive School: A Sourcebook for Developing Collaborative Groups* and Senge, (1990), *The Fifth Discipline: The Art and Practice of the Learning Organization*).

Pausing, a powerful tool improving emotional intelligence, is especially useful in meetings. Because teachers are always short on time, discussions at meetings can seem more like an Olympic ping-pong game than an opportunity to discuss and solve problems. We try to wait 3–5 seconds after a colleague speaks, so we can process and understand what he or she has said. Associated with the research on "wait time" exhibited by master teachers in the classroom, pausing relates to higher level thinking skills. At your next staff meeting, practice just this one norm. Although it is challenging, it improves the level of discussion.

Paraphrasing is the most powerful tool for reaching understanding and de-escalating conflict. The Adaptive Schools Organization (www.adaptiveschools.org) stresses not using the word "I" when paraphrasing another person. "What I hear you are saying is … ," is more about you and not the person speaking. Alternatives that move the focus to the speaker include, "So what you are saying is … ," or "So, the emotions you are feeling are …" I have used this skill numerous times when calming frustrated parents or coaching staff members.

Probing for specificity is digging deeper to really understand what a person is saying, thinking, or feeling. I usually use a "softener" and ask permission before probing for specificity. For example, "May I explore this a little further with you?" or "I sense your frustration here, but can you please share with me why you are so frustrated?"

Putting ideas on the table requires courage on the part of the speaker as well as acceptance, trust, and openness on the part of the group; if a culture encourages such behaviors, the power of synergy can create change. A strategy for this is "first turn-last turn." As we go around the table, everyone in turn adds a comment, thought, or idea. Use this power tool when you have one or two people dominating a conversation or meeting.

Paying attention to self and others is the essence of emotional intelligence. We need to be aware of and sensitive to everyone around the table. Although we may not agree with each other, we are committed to one another.

Presuming positive intentions is perhaps the most important and valuable norm in creating a high-functioning team and developing emotional intelligence. When we assure ourselves that no one will do anything to intentionally hurt us, we view things much differently, without fear. Chapter 6 discusses this strategy in detail.

Balancing advocacy and inquiry is the last norm. Emotionally intelligent people care as much about what others are thinking and feeling as they do about advocating for their own thoughts and feelings. When a leader really starts to inquire into the thoughts, ideas, and feelings of others, a powerful culture emerges.

Honoring the seven norms enables our school staff to engage in some great dialogue. When visitors come to staff meetings or professional development activities, they often share their amazement at how we openly, respectfully disagree with one another while debating or problem solving. Many schools have an "artificial harmony" of getting along with each other because they never openly engage in discussing controversies or disagreements. Highly functioning teams can debate and disagree respectfully.

Be patient and give a timeline. During a faculty meeting before the start of a school year, John, a new principal, introduced a schedule increasing students' academic time. In past years, teachers had built the schedule and forwarded it to the principal. The former schedule allotted teachers 45-minute lunches (the teacher contract stipulated a minimum 30 minutes for lunch) and assigned no duties during their planning periods, which allowed for most teachers to grade papers or check e-mail. A major paradigm shift for the faculty was that planning time would now involve collaborating with peers in teams to share successful teaching strategies and analyze student work as they built a professional learning community, an important initiative of the new principal.

As soon as John communicated the plans, strategies, and vision of a new professional learning community, several teachers appeared to become frustrated and agitated. But John recognized their fear and communicated to the staff that fear is normal during the change process. John quickly shared how it took his previous building three years to become a professional learning community. Because he shared his perspective on the time line, teachers could realize that they would have time to get used to the changes and grow into them, and they were "normal" not being comfortable with the idea yet.

When principals initiate professional learning communities, they usually find that some teachers who prefer working by themselves rather than as a member of a team, and some prefer working only with children. Others have no urge for further refinement or developing new skills. With such variables along with normal resistance, anger, fear, and sometimes even disrespect, the task of reform is challenging indeed. Principals need to remember, as John did, that nearly every teacher is a dedicated, compassionate, professional educator. Never losing sight of this, John strived for a balance of persistence and patience during the implementation stages. He was patient because he understood the fear associated with change. He knew that for many people change is loss, and people actually have to go through a grieving process. So John displayed empathy and was sympathetic when he listened to concerns. However, persistently sharing research and data that supported the initiative, he is converting more and more faculty to his vision along the way. Now, several years later, teachers at John's high-performing school embrace the concept of professional learning communities. In fact, the teachers build time for collaboration into the schedule. The strategies of being patient, sharing a timeline, being empathic about fear of change, but insistent on following the research-backed initiative are keys to success.

Control the temperature. Any school leader who overlooks the emotions of his or her staff and pushes on with a reform plan of the principal's own choosing, will indeed face failure. Heifetz and Linsky (2002) referred to the important skill of "controlling the temperature," or "monitoring the thermostat." When the school leader senses the emotions are rising, he or she needs to reclaim responsibility for tough issues by taking some responsibility away from the staff, establishing structure and roles, and addressing technical issues causing problems. During this time the school leader displays empathy and balances persistence with patience. When the temperature begins to lower, the school leader can once again give people responsibility in their comfort range, draw attention to tough issues, and bring conflicts to the surface.

Michele, the principal of a progressive middle school, demonstrated such leadership. For two years during professional development time , Michele trained her teachers to use a new data management system to load assessments and use the system to grade, store, and sort data that would help identify students needing intervention. It was a great tool that really contributed to the school's success. Unbeknownst to Michele, the district, excited about her building results, decided to integrate a district-wide data management system—a different system! So when teachers returned to school and learned that they were no longer able to use the system on which they had trained, frustration was rampant. Teachers' stress level quickly rose with beginning-of-the-year activities, the reloading of their assessments onto a new system, and responsibility for new intervention planning. But Michele was reading the temperature. She quickly assumed responsibility for getting district personnel to reload all the assessments, and Michele scanned and ran all of the teachers' reports for the entire year. After the first half of the year, when the teachers felt comfortable and organized with the new intervention program, Michelle organized training sessions for them to learn the new data system. By the end of the year more than half of the staff had trained on the new system, and the rest trained during the summer. Michele had her hand on the thermostat, and when she sensed the temperature was getting hot, she turned it down until things stabilized. Not only is temperature control an important concept for administrators to learn, but once teachers understand the concept, they can communicate when they are feeling stressed. Teachers in our building will actually use this as a "coaching cue" and alert me when I may need to check the temperature.

Have realistic expectations. The school leader who thinks leading school reform will be easy and without emotions is over-romanticizing the world. Although he knew it was unrealistic, Rick nevertheless expected his teachers to jump on board and express excitement whenever he talked about his expectations and goals for the school. He described his frequent response to his staff:

> I get that "what-do-you-mean; you don't understand kind of attitude." If I don't orally respond, I think my eyebrows or non-verbal behavior show it. I'm thinking, this is a great idea … trust me!

He went on to share he translated the staff's fear and concern into the thought that his staff was trying to derail or sabotage the initiative. Rick began to understand the fear and anger his staff experienced during stages of change had little relationship to his leadership. However, the way he reacted to their fear and anger spoke volumes about his leadership. His reaction communicated that their feelings were illogical and that he did not care about how they felt. His staff was not sabotaging his change efforts; he was—by not understanding the emotions of others.

Allow staff to have their emotions. Many principals do not display negative emotions when asked to do a job—and they expect their staffs to act accordingly. Such leaders can be blindsided when staff show fear or discontent or become upset with decisions. My experience shows that many times when school leaders pick up on fear, anger, or sadness from teachers, they associate this with a lack of commitment from the staff causing the leaders to react negatively. They then spend more time sorting out the fact that the teachers' emotions were not equal to their commitment and then making up with the staff than they would have by just acknowledging emotions and moving forward. After reflection and concentrated effort on improving their emotional intelligence, school leaders can understand this chain of reactions and change their behaviors to reflect this new understanding. Fear, anger, and sadness are feelings that all people have, and expressing them is a right of staff as long as they are expressed appropriately.

Any discomfort with those feelings that leaders have is their own problem. Never underestimate the value and importance of understanding the emotions of others.

➤ Questions for reflection

1. Think about a time when staff members may have thought you did not understand their emotions. Was this true? What could you have done to change those perceptions?

2. Have you ever been in a situation when someone did not understand how you were feeling? What were your thoughts at the time about this person? Is this how you want people to perceive you? What can you do to ensure that people know you are trying to understand their emotions?

3. Can you identify staff members in your building who are compliant rather than committed? Do you treat those people differently? When was the last time you addressed noncompliance in your building? How did you address the noncompliance?

➤ Steps to improve your emotional awareness of others

1. Observe others in the workplace. Study their facial expressions, body language, and voices.

2. During an event at work try to be aware of what others are feeling. Do not be afraid to ask questions to confirm your perceptions.

3. After an event, compare observations with a colleague about others' emotions.

4. Try to walk in another person's shoes. Try to experience how that person feels.

Chapter 5

Emotions: A Source of Information

Even when technical data drives a final decision, the emotional information around that decision can have immense impact on a principal's communication and implementation of the decision.

Every day principals make decisions, hundreds per day, five days a week. To make many of those decisions, information must be gathered quickly from a variety of sources. Today's schools are more data-driven than ever. When examining data, what information do principals gather about emotions? As mentioned earlier, refusing to acknowledge the emotions of those around you, including parents, teachers, and students, sets you up for a nonproductive tenure as a school leader.

Balancing technical and emotional information

The development of national and state standards for school principals has narrowed the focus of the skills and abilities required for successful and effective school leaders. Principals must collect, sort, and analyze data from assessments, feedback, processes, piloted programs, and implementation of new strategies. There is a tremendous pressure on principals to focus on state data, surveys, and achievement scores. While using hard data from these sources is paramount in creating successful schools, principals who ignore emotional information and fail to acknowledge the stress, fear, and anxiety associated with reform, new initiatives, and mandates will have little success in cultivating a culture of trust and commitment.

The principal in the following scenario piloted full inclusion in social studies and science classes collecting data to support her position of using a full inclusion model throughout the school. Michele, the principal, has always been an advocate of full inclusion—placing students, regardless of their needs or disabilities, in regular classrooms with their peers. Although the social studies and science teachers had a more challenging year than usual, the student value-added and student achievement data showed the special education students were learning more in full inclusion social studies and science classrooms than in math and reading special education classes. The data were strong enough to support Michele's advocacy for inclusion, and she met with teachers at the year's end to plan implementing inclusion schoolwide the following year.

At the meeting, Michele listened as teachers expressed their concerns and their fears of moving from their traditional process of separating students with physical, mental, or behavioral challenges from regular classrooms. Although their students on IEPs in the pilot inclusion classes learned more than they had in years past, it was obvious that all of the teachers were scared, nervous, and even angry. The more teachers shared their frustrations and concerns, the more Michele listened. Many teachers lacked confidence in teaching students with special needs; all of them agreed it would be much more difficult to teach a variety of ability levels in their classrooms. Michele presumed positive intentions and knew deep down she did not have to convince teachers of the ethics of inclusion. She knew her priority at the time was not to influence, advocate or debate, but rather just to listen. When the meeting's designated ending time arrived, Michele thanked the teachers for sharing their concerns and expressing their feelings. But Michele said it was her responsibility to ensure high levels of learning for all students, and given the success of the pilot, the school would implement full inclusion the following year.

Next Michele asked the teachers to write their hopes and goals for all of the special education students in the building and what their vision was for full inclusion in their school. By focusing on the staff's hopes and vision, by introducing data that showed the special education students did learn more in a full inclusion environment, and by acknowledging the emotional information associated with the challenge of changing, Michele led the teachers in planning the successful implementation of a full inclusion model. As she collected the emotional data by listening carefully to her teachers, Michele realized how much she would need to support, encourage, and coach them through this process. Had Michele ignored the emotional data and underestimated the fear and resistance to the change, implementation of the model may have failed due to lack of buy-in from the teachers.

Data from thousands of professionals taking the Genos Emotional Intelligence Assessment reveal that the most successful leaders do not have the highest scores. Thus, those people tending to make decisions based solely on emotional information are less likely to succeed. However, a balance between technical and emotional data collection and analyses may be the key to successfully implementing school reform initiatives. In the previous story, Michele knew what the right decision was. She also knew it was important to take in as much emotional information as she could to successfully plan for the implementation of full inclusion. By hearing and understanding the staff's level of fear associated with full inclusion, she could organize professional development and support around this new initiative. During the year, the teachers did struggle and it was challenging. But at the end of the school year when the student data came back with higher-than-ever scores for students with disabilities and special needs, the school celebrated. The teachers realized their work was worth it.

Had Michele bailed out on her plan to implement a full inclusion model on emotional information alone, the students would have lost. Balancing information from technical data and emotional information is an art. There are times when emotional information may outweigh technical data. However, more times than not, principals fail to collect emotional data for fear of being accused of soliciting information and then not listening. Principals must collect all sorts of data, including emotional information. Even when hard data drives a final decision, the emotional information around that decision has immense impact on a principal's communication and implementation of the decision.

Don't assume others see your logic

Your emotional intelligence quotient will be most on display when the school community's reaction to a decision you've made may seem illogical, simplistic, or overblown. In one coaching session, Chip, who serves as an athletic director/ assistant principal, shared a story of a decision he made concerning a football game.

> I had football coaches come to me and ask if they could play their football games at our junior high field rather than our high school field. They said with all of the rain and the number of events that we have had on our high school field, it is in terrible condition. But the junior high field does not have the concession stands, the seating capacity, indoor plumbing, restrooms, and the advertising on our scoreboards that people paid for. This is what I explained to the football coaches.

Because he had listened to the coaches, sympathized with them, and explained his reasons for denying use of the junior high field, Chip was frustrated that the coaches, when they talked to parents, created the perception that he did not care about the football team. Although Chip made a logical, reasoned decision, it was unpopular with the football team and parents. Part of the responsibility of being emotionally intelligent is not expecting that our every decision will win approval. We must and will make unpopular decisions.

Reinforce the importance of feelings

Using emotional information does not mean school leaders must abandon logic or well-thought-out plans and make decisions based on their emotions or the emotions of others. It means that the more school leaders make decisions based on hard data, the greater the opportunity for staff members to develop the perceptions that you do not care about them or their input, only data. When making decisions, school leaders must do their best to listen, educate, and inform others. Never undervalue the emotions of others, but make decisions based on well-organized plans or lead collaborative groups in the decision-making progress.

After he had made a decision that he thought was well-reasoned, a school leader became frustrated and angry when he heard that a teacher assigned to a duty as part of the "fallout" of his decision was upset. The school leader stated:

Before learning about the value of emotional intelligence, I may have even sent an e-mail justifying why I moved the computers and that this was the way it was going to be. But instead, I went to the teacher. I asked her to explain how she felt. I explained to her I understood why she would feel this way, and that I did not mean to hurt her feelings and that I was sorry her feelings were hurt. I explained why I moved the computers and why I also had to assign a duty period. The fact that I took the time to seek her out, ask her how she felt, express how I felt and why I chose to move the computers really made a difference.

Following up with staff members is cultivating the garden. Acknowledging the validity of her feelings helped the teacher move forward and accept the decision, helped heal the rift between principal and teacher, and cultivated cooperation in the computer lab instead of a potential "weed in the garden."

Questions for reflection

1. What percentages of your decisions are made on technical data rather than emotional data? With which decisions are you more comfortable?

2. Think about the emotions of your staff the last time you made a decision based on hard data. Were they supportive of your decision? Did you care about your staff's emotions during the decision-making process?

3. When would you ever allow emotional information to outweigh the importance of technical or hard data in making a decision? When would you allow technical or hard data to outweigh the importance of emotional information in making a decision?

Steps to improve your emotional reasoning

1. Ask others about their feelings about a decision you need to make. Ask them to differentiate between their gut feelings and what is really the best decision to make.

2. Explore your own feelings regarding a decision you have to make. Are you making the decision based on technical (hard) data or on emotions?

3. Make a list of decisions you make at work; beside the items on the list estimate how much emotional information and how much technical data go into the decisions.

Chapter 6
Emotional Self-Management

> Every morning when I walk into my office, I am wondering what details were not taken care of last night or what e-mail is waiting for me. I just try to get through the day without any catastrophes. It's like dealing with fear every day. —School Leader

A rather obvious but under-recognized truth is that effectively managing one's own emotions can improve job satisfaction and enhance performance. The life of a school leader is filled with role conflicts and strains. The stress associated with this position, which requires long hours and results sometimes in little appreciation, has led to many state organizations predicting major shortages of principals in the near future. Despite a rise in salaries, emotional stress, including lack of appreciation and burnout, is contributing to the impending shortage. This chapter will give you some tools and strategies to increase your job satisfaction, reduce your stress, and improve your quality of life.

Managing your emotions vs. emotional self-control

Although the Emotional Self-Management (managing emotions) dimension is similar to the Emotional Self-Control dimension of the Genos EI Model, the main difference is that managing your emotions includes how you respond after tense emotional events or conflict and whether you can maintain a positive mood and continued effectiveness. Emotional self-control is the controlling of your own emotions at the time you perceive a threat. When principals learn how to manage their emotions, they increase their interpersonal effectiveness and quality of life. The school day does not usually end after one emotional situation, and even though you may have handled yourself well at the time, you must bring your "A game" the rest of the day. Further, when you go home after a tough day, your loved ones deserve a spouse, partner, or parent that can focus on the needs and pleasures of the family.

Many principals report themselves as effective in controlling their emotions during the time they are dealing with a person, group, or an intense event. However, *afterward,* their inability to manage their emotions creates adverse effects including poor encounters with another person or group, mood changes during the day, and lack of productivity for the remainder of the work day. Nearly every principal I have worked with individually or in groups has also admitted being short-tempered with someone in their personal lives because of an event that had happened many hours before at work. Learning to understand and manage emotions will have a positive effect on nearly every aspect of your life, and failure to manage emotions effectively can not only be detrimental to your quality of life but to your health as well. Numerous studies link chronic stress to aging, disease, and death.

The snowball effect of unmanaged emotions. Principals who have little understanding of their emotions and even less skill in managing them often feel unappreciated and get trapped in one emotional crisis after another. When dealing with a crisis or an intense situation at work, have you ever suddenly realized you have become withdrawn, moody, and short with other people? When principals do not take the time to sort out their thoughts or reflect on their emotions during an emotional event, they are often caught in an energy trap the remainder of the day. An administrator reported how a particularly bad morning affected the remainder of his day.

> Today was not such a great ending. For some reason I allowed the fact that a teacher continued to ask me questions about a decision I made make me angry and mad. Next, I reacted emotionally to another staff member.

Even though he demonstrated some emotional self-control by not reacting negatively to the teacher questioning his decision, his poor emotional self-management prevented him from allowing the incident to affect the remainder of the day.

Strategies for managing your emotions

This part of Chapter 6 may be the most important part of the book as we explore in some detail many strategies that will help you improve your emotional intelligence. There is no one best strategy, so think of each as a tool to be placed in your emotional intelligence toolbox. As you work on your development goals, practice these strategies. Eventually, you may find one or two "go to" strategies that you use most often when feeling emotionally challenged.

The power of positive intentions. Presuming positive intentions, one of the collaborative norms discussed earlier, is also an excellent strategy for managing and controlling your emotions. While this strategy is powerful for helping control one's emotions, it also happens to be my number one tool for managing my emotions.

Here are some examples of how it works. After an event or incident in which a person successfully controls his or her emotions, the person begins to reflect, or maybe even "cool down," even though throughout the whole incident, the person may not have shown any outward emotions. It is important to begin reflecting immediately after an event. Try to use the power of positive intentions in your reflection; try to honestly look at the event from another's point of view as if they had a positive purpose, a genuine question, or concern.

Each of the following incidents provoked a negative emotion and reaction from a principal who then shared the experience during a coaching session. Following each incident, the bold type shows how the principal could have used positive intentions to prevent the negative reaction.

1. An angry phone call or e-mail from a parent in the community: **The intention was that the parent wanted me to hear firsthand his frustration, and out of respect, he chose to contact me directly.**

2. A call from the superintendent inquiring about an event that happened in a building, after you thought you had successfully handled it: **The superintendent must have received a call from the parent involved and just wants to touch base so he can honestly let the parent know that you had talked together about it.**

3. A meeting with a teacher and an official from the teachers' union: **The teacher really wanted to come to an agreement or consensus without writing a grievance.**

4. Without first talking with you, a meeting occurs between a teacher and the superintendent to discuss a concern about a situation in the building. **The**

teacher did not want to disappoint me or was afraid that she might get overly emotional if she talked to me first.

These are just four examples of how presuming positive intentions can enable a principal to prevent emotions from causing them to behave ineffectively. Learning to manage your emotions contributes to overall life satisfaction.

Pausing. Although the value of pausing is commonly recognized, you would be surprised how many principals share with me that if they had just stopped and thought about how they were going to respond for a few seconds, they would have handled themselves differently.

Basically, pausing allows you to consider whether or not the amygdala has indeed sacrificed accuracy for speed. Is the event really a threat or life threatening? The key is to develop a habit that will enable you to exercise pausing. Some principals have gone to just calling it the five-second pause and during this time do a Stop-Look-Listen activity and try to figure out what emotions they are experiencing and why. To ensure I pause five seconds, especially when I am in larger groups, I bring one of my hands to my chin to suggest and demonstrate that I am in a "thinking mode." This really helps me in two areas. First, it allows me to Pause and Stop-Look-Listen, and second it allows me to really process what the other person is saying. If someone else is overly emotional, your pausing and listening rather than responding too quickly can defuse the situation helping both you and the other person.

What would you suggest to a colleague? One good tool is to remove yourself immediately from a situation and imagine it is happening to someone else, much like using a case study. Often if you remove yourself from an emotionally-charged situation and the emotions associated with it, you would be able to give great advice to a colleague. Now what is important is to follow your own advice. An example of this strategy is given in Chapter 8.

Question yourself and ask for proof. Where is the proof that this is truly happening? Has there ever been a situation like this before where you had some of the same feelings and beliefs and you were wrong? By asking yourself these two questions, you are assessing the accuracy of the perceived threat.

Probe for specificity. When you take time to pause and ask yourself questions about what you are thinking or feeling, you are truly probing for specificity. However, you can also use this as a strategy when someone else is emotionally hijacked. By probing for specificity you can help another person truly separate their thoughts from their emotions. A similar strategy is "Balancing Advocacy and Inquiry." When you really pause and take the time to probe into what people are feeling or thinking, you are well on your way of becoming an excellent principal. You can use some other strategies and ask, "Where is the truth?" or ask them if they are presuming positive intentions during this time. Many of the strategies advanced in this book can be used to help your staff during conflict or emotional times.

Exercise, nutrition, rest. Exercise, nutrition, and rest have to be included in any list of strategies for controlling your emotions. Some administrators exercise before going home, and they have increased their health, well-being, and relationships at home. Others plan their days and practice reflection during morning workouts. Still others use reading, painting, playing video games, or doing needlepoint as a productive strategy for dealing with their emotion-filled days. Whatever the method, it is important to find one that works for you—and schedule time to do it.

Nutrition and rest are usually the first two areas sacrificed when principals move from their relaxed summers to their tense school years. Because of their busy schedules, many principals are challenged by maintaining proper nutrition. If you are nutritionally challenged, read a book detailing proper nutrition and diet's positive effect on your life. Keep a journal of what you are eating along with your emotional intelligence journal and look for a relationship between your diet and your emotional ups and downs. Learning how to manage your emotions will help you rest and sleep better, and adequate rest and sleep will help you successfully manage your emotions.

Why manage your emotions?

Simply to create a better you—one who will be more productive, have a greater influence on staff, be able to cultivate a committed culture, and improve your school as well as every other aspect of your personal and professional life. I tell people that I have the very best job in the world. I get up every day and look forward to going to school to be with adults as well as children. I could not always have said this, but after completing emotional intelligence training and practicing the skills involved, I became much more relaxed. People did not question my decisions because they did not like me; they questioned me because they needed more clarification. When parents call and ask questions, it is not because they do not trust me or the school; it is because they want to be involved. There are many reasons for beginning today to develop and hone your emotional intelligence skills, if not for the sole reason that you want to enjoy your job more. Better health, better relationships, and less stress are just a few benefits of high emotional intelligence.

Emotional intelligence at home and school. Some administrators may think they can practice high emotional intelligence at school but not at home. Sam is principal of a junior high that produces excellent results in academics and athletics. Working 60–70 hours per week and visible at nearly every school function, Sam has the reputation for being fair, patient, understanding, and a very good listener. There may not be a better principal around. However, as a husband and father, Sam used to lack patience and understanding at home. In fact, Sam was a different person at work than at home. Allowing the role strain from a very difficult job to affect his home and marriage, Sam managed his emotions very poorly and lashed out at his wife and children. When Sam began developing his emotional intelligence, he wanted most to learn how to manage his emotions. By practicing reflection, presuming positive intentions, and using other strategies found here, Sam said he "felt like a new man."

Managing emotions in your different roles. Brent, a principal with three small children at home, is constantly challenged with managing his emotions. Sometimes a frustrating morning getting the kids off to school and daycare leads to poor interactions with his staff at school, and when he has a stress-free morning at home and something happens at school, he displays very little patience with his children. Carrying anger, frustration, and stress in this vicious cycle of home to school and school to home has taken its toll not only on Brent but also on his staff and family. When writing and identifying goals for improving your emotional intelligence, be sure to include goals for practicing emotional intelligence at home.

Managing emotions when you change roles

The goal is to be emotionally intelligent in all aspects of your life and in all roles you play that will bring better life satisfaction and enjoyment to yourself and those around you. However, sometimes role strain results as we try to balance the requirements of our different roles. Following is a case study of an administrator balancing the role of assistant principal and athletic director.

Chip, an assistant principal and athletic director, was most passionate about helping lead his school to excellence; but his athletic director's position required 75 percent of his school time (and sometimes four evenings a week). Thirty-two-year-old Chip was quite likeable. As a teacher he formed strong relationships with both students and teachers, and during his last year of teaching, the school's yearbook had been dedicated to him. Unfortunately, as the new school assistant principal and athletic director, Chip had not been able to develop the same kind of relationships that he had enjoyed during his tenure as a teacher.

Relationships with teachers who had formerly been his friends changed. Students no longer viewed him as a student-friendly teacher. Although he was still excited about the opportunity to be a school leader, daily interactions and relationships with parents, teachers, and students challenged his leadership skills.

Relationships changed at home as well, as Chip had limited time to spend with his family, who saw Chip become a different person under the stress of his new position. Chip regretted the change at home saying:

> Before I changed positions, I was closer to my son than my wife was. Recently my son said, "Dad, you don't do things with me anymore." This was hard to hear. Now he is closer to my wife, and I see it. This is not a bad thing, but it is tough.

So, Chip's challenges were to handle a dual work positions with the majority of his time spent on his least desirable role, a change in peer and student relationships, and changes in roles at home. Who wouldn't struggle under this weight?

After reviewing results of his personal and staff emotional intelligence assessments, Chip was able to identify that managing and controlling his emotions were his two areas of greatest opportunity for development. Of the assessments, Chip said:

> It was nice to have time to go back over the report again and the initial shock. You're right, at first I thought, did I pass or did I fail? When I was new to my new job, I thought I had to be tough, or have an image of toughness to establish myself. Which I think is probably false. I think I tried to come off tougher than I am, just like a teacher at the beginning of the school year. Even though I was now supervising adults instead of children, I did not want them to walk over me.

This perspective led to behaviors such as working very hard to control his emotions and not reveal them. When people questioned his decisions and made negative comments based on erroneous information or rumors, Chip had to expend much energy to keep his emotions in check. These poorly managed emotions, stresses, and challenges of the new position had definitely decreased the ratio of positive to negative encounters with adults and students. The increase in negative encounters only led to more stress, which led to more negative interactions with others.

Chip added during one of our sessions:

I need to worry less about the perception (of being tough) and let people in. I need to do a better job of expressing myself when talking to staff and students. I need to consider my own and others' feelings when making decisions. I need to remain calm and positive when dealing with conflict and difficult situations.

Chip also entered in his journal, "What I want most out of this program is the ability to develop and nurture better personal relationships with those that I work with."

Get control of your life today

To start living your life without stress and fear is impossible, but you can learn to live with less stress by managing your emotions. What is your first thought when:

- the administrative assistant tells you a parent is on the phone for you?
- the superintendent stops by unexpectedly?
- you see an e-mail has arrived from a parent?
- you are called out of your office to a classroom?
- you walk into the office and a parent is waiting to see you?

Because we have all had the experiences above, we likely assign negative emotions to these events every time they happen—even before we know how they are going to turn out. However, with emotional intelligence training and an effort to reshape our pre-existing mental models, we can began living and enjoying our lives and jobs again. Now when I get phone calls from parents, I no longer make negative assumptions, and most of the time I am pleasantly surprised by the conversations. Indeed, a majority of my phone conversations have always been positive, and I wonder why I ever associated negative emotions or fears with such calls. E-mails are the same way. When you open e-mails and try to find good and positive intentions in the text, you will be surprised at how positive they actually are. The same can be said with other aspects of your job. Now I am not suggesting being naïve and overly romantic about the world in which we live and work, but I encourage you to use the strategies in this chapter and start living a richer life today.

Questions for reflection

1. Do you bring stress, frustration and anger home? What does this look like? Does any of the stress you experience at work take away from your happiness?
2. Describe the emotions that create your biggest challenges in being productive. Which emotions cause you the greatest stress?

Steps to improve your emotional self-management

1. Try to identify your different emotions at work. Identify emotions that lead to negative feelings or negative moods. Identify emotions that lead to positive moods.
2. Understand that emotions usually drive thoughts and behavior. Think about some behaviors or feelings you would like to change. Identify the emotions associated with those behaviors and thoughts.

Chapter 7

Managing Others' Emotions

Very few school leaders lack confidence, verbal skills, or the ability to influence. However, time and time again we hear that school leaders are not good listeners … the more times you do take time to listen and acknowledge others' feelings, most people will be able to understand your reasoning and follow your lead even if you make an unpopular decision.

Most people seeking improvement in emotional intelligence usually consider only the skill of managing their own emotions. However, leaders that can understand and manage the emotions of others have a powerful tool for leveraging extraordinary commitment and performance from their staffs. And just like the other dimensions of emotional intelligence, you can develop and refine this skill.

In addition to generating greater performance from others, managing the emotions of others enables you to create a positive work environment and effectively deal with conflict in the workplace. The inability to deal effectively with conflict is a common weakness of many school leaders. A popular joke is that the last class a school leader takes before becoming licensed is the class in which the spine is removed. Hypotheses abound about the reason for school leaders' difficulties in dealing with others' emotions, but I think it is usually caused by a lack of organizational awareness rather than a lack of concern for others' emotions. Intensely focused on whatever task is at hand, some principals fail to carve out time for dealing with emotions and sensitive issues. Leaders who are not aware of emotions and do not want to be aware of emotions are essentially isolated in a position of little organizational awareness.

Leading your staff to greater performance

Two basic human needs are 1) the need to be loved and 2) the need to know we are "enough." When leaders take the time to be sincerely aware of and understanding of their staffs' emotions, teachers feel that their leaders care about them and will be loyal and committed.

Patience and persistence. After completing her first year as principal, Elizabeth, a master at balancing patience and persistence, was ready to challenge her staff with implementing short cycle assessments, end-of-year assessments, additional interventions, and a new philosophy of relentlessly educating all children. Elizabeth's passion for excellence was refreshing for some but intimidating for others. Many of the faculty expressed concerns that she was overestimating their students' real potential, that their community did not highly value education, that not all students were ready to learn, and that many kids today were just different and impossible to reach.

After listening, Elizabeth affirmed her high confidence in the abilities of the faculty based on her year of watching them teach and build relationships with their students. Elizabeth stressed that the futures of their children depended on the level of learning that would take place within their school and that her hope was that every student would have the opportunity to be successful. Without a commitment to excellence and extra intervention for students, many of them would not have the opportunity for success. Elizabeth was appealing to her teachers' commitment to helping all children learn.

Some of the body language (dropping heads, slouching shoulders, rolling eyes) and some previous conversations with staff members told Elizabeth that there was fear in the room. Empathizing with her staff, she validated their fear and worries about the changes and then asked them to worry about the children's futures as well.

Unafraid of openly recognizing some common emotions that prevent change, Elizabeth instead focused on the hope of achievement to inspire and instill courage in her staff. Stressing that together they could develop a school that would not allow failure, she helped them envision a school in which every student could learn in an environment of mutual support and understanding.

Key to Elizabeth's message was her sincerity. Quick to perceive insincerity, a faculty feeling manipulated by a "let's win one for the Gipper" speech will lose motivation. In fact, my experience working with leaders has shown that often the most verbal principals who speak with the most eloquence during speeches and pep talks are viewed by their staffs as manipulative. Elizabeth was giving more than a pep talk. She was emphasizing the great struggle that lay ahead, making it clear she would also face challenges caused by the changes. By assuring their staffs that they, too, will be challenged during the change process, principals can build enough support to launch reform initiatives.

While responding to the emotions of her staff, Elizabeth remained committed to sharing her vision of every student's achieving success. A principal with a high level of emotional intelligence, Elizabeth managed the emotions of her staff by channeling their energy in a positive direction.

Creating a positive work environment

Elizabeth had mastered one of the most important concepts in managing others' emotions. Although it was not prevalent during the meeting, much of Elizabeth's work had been done behind the scenes and informally. Whether it was during lunch, a conference time, or an after-school talk, Elizabeth probed for specificity about what emotions the staff was experiencing as she communicated the new vision.

More important, Elizabeth delved deeper into the thinking of the staff that led to their emotions: "Why would you be angry if we started using more planning time for conferencing?" "What is the main source of the fear?" "Do you really think if you failed, you would lose your job?" By such probing, Elizabeth was able to discover some unproductive thought patterns that she could address and refute.

One was that the change would set teachers up for failure resulting in reprimands or even replacement. Elizabeth also learned that a decade earlier many of the staff had experienced their principal spending time, money, and resources to launch a somewhat similar initiative. When it failed due to lack of spending on professional development and implementation support, the teachers were blamed for a lack of commitment. Teachers well remembered how this felt for when emotions are evoked, people don't forget. Because she had worked to understand the reasons for the staff's hesitation, Elizabeth could dispel unfounded fears. After she felt well-versed on the thoughts and emotions of her staff, Elizabeth began to expand on communicating her vision and communicating hope and the emotions associated with the eventual successful attainment of the goals.

Another administrator, Doug, really wanted to improve his skills of managing others' emotions. Having learned to recognize when he was about to be emotionally hijacked, he would take quick action. Doug had learned to leverage his strengths to help others. Doug's journal entry about a meeting with a teacher who was upset about a decision he made is an example:

> Today when dealing with a teacher over a particularly nagging issue that I had dealt with several times, I tried to relate to the way she felt. I listened carefully to her, made it clear that I understood fully how she felt, and then explained the reason the decision was made.

The teacher appreciated the opportunity for discussing the decision calmly and quietly and left feeling much better. Many times we can help people manage their emotions simply by giving them an outlet, just listening, or answering questions.

Doug also said the emotional intelligence coaching improved his ability to deal with concerned parents:

> There is nothing more important to a parent than his or her child. When I really understand this, I am not surprised when a parent is irrational or does not see the logic in a decision. A parent's behavior is no longer a trigger, because I know it is not because he or she does not trust me.

Doug mentioned in meetings with parents he listens more, and, when they are done talking, he asks whether together they can do some problem solving to resolve the issue.

Leading change and dealing with crises

Learning to manage others' emotions is crucial in leading change or dealing with a crisis. Having just taken a new job, one school leader was shocked to see the group become emotional during her first department meeting. She had brought the entire staff of 17 together for a meeting to discuss one urgent item, two minor issues of a fundraiser, and some electrical work for their building. Displaying a wide range of emotions, her staff complained about the rewiring project and went on to become very upset about a fundraiser which they themselves had suggested and committed to run. She said:

> I really never got to the main part of the agenda because so many people were complaining or commenting on the fundraiser and rewiring project. I became really frustrated.

In spite of her frustration that the meeting was not productive and everyone was off task, she understood the staff needed to vent, and she needed to be empathetic and listen. After a short time of listening to the frustrations of the staff, she recommended that the group put the fundraiser on hold and revisit the decision later. Everyone seemed relieved with this decision. Sometimes, leadership is that simple. Although the school leader felt blamed for the staff's fundraiser idea, she realized that being a supportive team member, listening to staff concerns, and helping develop a new money-generating strategy was far more important than winning an argument and saving face. She said, "Yes, I was angry, but the importance of building a team that could communicate with me was the highest priority." High in emotional intelligence, she successfully managed others' emotions.

Jim Collins in his book *Good to Great* (2001) stated that great companies did more with their "not to do" lists than their "to do" lists. Not only are "not to do" lists important for leading, but also, to go fast there are times you must go slowly. However, leadership is not always so simple, and sometimes in spite of negative emotions associated with a project or initiative, the leader must go on. But taking the time to understand the swirl of emotions allows the group to better prepare for obstacles that may occur later in the project. Just as important as listening to the emotions is identifying the underlying cause of the emotions, which usually takes the most time.

Ed, a principal, was working on managing others' emotions. His trigger for anger is when people attempt to disguise their selfishness as "doing what's best for kids." In a talk with a staff member about what the concerns would be for having common assessments or short cycle assessments, the teacher replied that the teachers were afraid of losing their autonomy. Ed said,

> They are not afraid of that! They are afraid of having to share some of their power as classroom teachers; they're afraid of having a measuring stick, and there's just a personal fear. Part of this goes back to that they do not trust administrators, which means they don't trust me.

When asked whether it was okay for his teachers to have this fear, Ed replied, "It is fine, and I understand the fear." I asked Ed:

> If you want to lead the staff to developing assessments and the teachers are really afraid, and it's ok for them to be afraid, and you know they are afraid, how can you help manage their emotions for increased effectiveness? What can you do next?

Ed answered:

> Try to move them beyond the fear. Explain that you understand the fear. But it's like they think our intentions are to divide and conquer or to reward people for mundane tasks. I just get so shocked and surprised by some of the reactions. So I have the staff openly express their fears, help them understand the normality of the fear, and offer support during this process.

Next Ed had to figure out how he could lead the initiative to develop and implement short cycle and common assessments. He thought the first step was that the administration had to earn the teachers' trust. I asked, "The trust of everyone?" Ed answered, "No." When asked how many staff members' trust he would have to earn to get this initiative on the way, Ed answered, "That's a tough number, it may be not how many, but it might be whose trust you earn." So I asked him to identify the staff he would need on board to champion such an effort. After he stated several names from the Math Department, we settled on piloting it with the Math Department and using the data, both qualitative and quantitative, and their leadership to champion the initiative for the rest of the building. "Go slow to go fast" is the piloting model.

What advice would you give another principal? Through reflection, Ed was able to solve his own problem and come up with his own ideas. This is the power of reflecting. Asking "What advice would you give to another administrator?" is another strategy I often use. When I look back at some of my mistakes in dealing with my own or others' emotions, I often find my choice or behavior was quite opposite the advice I would have given a colleague or client. So, I have taught myself to use one of the collaborative norms we talked about earlier that is also a great emotional intelligence strategy: I pause for about 5 seconds. During this time I ask myself what advice I would give to someone else in this situation. You need not be a coach to use this strategy. Sometimes by just removing yourself from the situation and thinking about someone else facing the same issue, you become less emotional, and can make a better decision.

Dealing with conflict

Emotionally intelligent leaders are great listeners. They understand that sometimes taking time to listen will complicate their already busy schedule, but showing people that you truly care by giving them the time they deserve pays off.

Sally has been a driven, task-oriented school leader for more than ten years. She keeps a work pace rivaling a world championship thoroughbred on Derby Day in Lexington, Kentucky. While preparing for a presentation on student achievement for the board of education, she had closed her office door for about 15 minutes when Billy Smith's mother and father arrived at school wanting to discuss a disciplinary action taken with their son the previous day. His teasing and bullying of other students had earned him an after-school detention. Although Sally really felt rushed to finish the board presentation, she knew she needed to make time for the parents.

Opening her office door, Sally came out to meet Billy and his parents and invite them into her office to sit informally with them at a round table. Sally reminded herself not to assume the parents would protest the detention, not to defend the discipline of the school, and not to immediately discuss Billy's discipline record. Sally listened to Billy and probed for specific reasons why he felt he was having trouble interacting with his peers.

Whenever the parents displayed anger at the school, Sally empathized by commenting that as a parent, she, too, would be very upset by the situation. Then, by reminding them that they were all on the same team, Sally would bring the parents back to the task at hand while directing the conversation toward finding solutions for Billy's behavior.

When the meeting finished almost an hour later, both parents thanked Sally for her time and left feeling satisfied with the outcome of the meeting. Billy still had his detention, and his parents knew the school was working with and not against them. Sally was glad that she had taken time to meet with the parents and that the meeting had been so productive, giving priority to her main responsibility of serving students and parents.

Balancing advocacy and inquiry. Although Sally has the verbal and analytical skills to win nearly every debate she enters, and her ability to influence has labeled her as someone that could sell "snow to Eskimos," she realized that most people just want the opportunity to be heard. In her early years, she would dominate the conversations and always had the last word. Sally began to notice that after several interactions with her, people would not come to her as often and started choosing her assistants as listeners.

Now, along with being a great listener, Sally has committed to the process of balancing advocacy and inquiry. Instead of solely advocating her ideas or suggestions, Sally takes the time to really hear and understand the ideas and suggestions of others. After everyone has had an opportunity to share, she usually concludes by saying "let's discuss what we think is the best idea or combine the suggestions to make a new idea." This conclusion reminds her and everyone else that she is not trying to get everyone to agree to her idea but to come up with the best decision.

Parents, teachers, and students now like to communicate with Sally. The keys to balancing advocacy and inquiry are to 1) Pause, 2) Listen, 3) Be aware of your and others' emotions, 4) Listen; avoid solving problems or giving advice immediately, 5) Paraphrase and ask for clarification, 6) Resolve the problem together. Meetings can become much more productive when shareholders really try to understand where other team members are coming from, thus the inquiry.

Very few school leaders lack confidence, verbal skills, or the ability to influence. However, time and time again we hear that school leaders are not good listeners. Of course in reality, school leaders are listening—at least some of the time. But recall from Chapter 5 that decision making is improved when you balancing technical data and emotional information. Once you make a decision not in agreement with someone else's position, they can and will sometimes assert, "You did not listen!" However, the more times you do take the time to listen and acknowledge others' feelings, most people will be able to understand your reasoning and follow your lead even if you make an unpopular decision.

Questions for reflection

1. Can you describe a time when you successfully managed the emotions of others? What did you do that was so successful? How did your staff respond? What were your emotions at the time?

2. Can you describe a time when you did not successfully manage the emotions of others? What did you do that limited your success to manage the emotions of others? Describe your emotions at the time.

3. Have you ever witnessed a mentor who was great at managing the emotions of others? What did they do differently from those who do not manage the emotions of others well? What skills do they have?

Steps to improving emotional management of others

1. Keep an emotional journal. Write down all of your work experiences of dealing with others during emotional times.

2. Observe others' emotions. Observe how people deal with those who are emotional. Make mental notes or notes in a journal about your observations.

3. Identify the actions or experiences that make you feel good at work. Practice applying these to others in the workplace.

4. Practice becoming a better active listener. Suspend your beliefs and paraphrase when possible.

Chapter 8
Emotional Self-Control

I became angry and scared when I got the e-mail.
I am tired of being underappreciated and second-guessed
by people. I let my emotions control my actions...

—A School Principal

Managing one's emotions and controlling them are slightly different. Emotional self-control (controlling emotions) is related to how you control your emotions or reactions when you perceive a threat. Emotional self-management has to do with how effectively you manage your stress and moods. Emotional self-control can be one of the most challenging dimensions of the emotional intelligence construct.

As is well known, it is easier to keep the peace than to restore it; but this may not be true when dealing with emotions. Unless we work hard at using our skills and strategies (Chapter 6) to understand our emotions, they can get the best of us. There is little hope for the principal who is not able to maintain stability in times of conflict or crisis. There are times when school leaders are yelled at, distrusted, ignored, talked about, and made to feel insignificant—and this by their own staffs! While I always believed that the classroom teacher's job is the most demanding and exhausting job in education, my experiences as a teacher, administrator, and school leaders' coach showed me that there is no job in education filled with more stress, frustration, and challenges than that of the school principal.

One of my professors used to say, "You have to have the skin of an armadillo and the heart of a marshmallow" to be an effective school leader. The armadillo skin symbolizes a level of protection to prevent your feelings from being hurt, which can cause you to overreact when emotional. A principal with the ability to maintain composure during emotional and intense situations will certainly gain the respect of a majority of staff members. Administrators regularly confirm the validity of the armadillo skin analogy and say that the thick skin develops as one serves as an administrator and that without it, they would have lost confidence and self-esteem. I caution you to not "protect or shield" yourself from your own emotions but rather to become a successful administrator by controlling your emotions.

Remember the principal at the beginning of Chapter 6 who became frustrated by a teacher who continued to ask questions? Thinking he was controlling his emotions because he did not overreact in a negative way, he later went on to react poorly to another colleague. Even though the principal thought he had his emotions under control, the fact that the emotions created a negative encounter later in the day indicated his lack of emotional control. Not overreacting to the first teacher was a good start, but not nearly enough. This is an example of the relationship between emotional self-control and emotional self-management. If the principal had assumed positive intentions, he might never have reached the point of having to control his response to the teacher, because he would never have gotten angry. Maybe the teacher just wanted more information or a better explanation for a decision that had been made.

When we know we are making decisions on the best information available and our own intentions are good, there is no need to be defensive when questioned. However, when we try to analyze or assume the worst when someone asks for clarification, we may have doubts or lack confidence, which can lead to anger, resentment, or fear. Many times it is our own nonproductive thought patterns that lead to negative emotions.

Nonproductive thought patterns

The following example shows how previously held thought patterns can prevent our brain cortex from using logic while allowing the aymgdala to trigger an emotion leading to a poor reaction.

I often ask educators at conferences, "What would be your first thoughts if the fire alarm went off. Fear? Stress?" Most educators respond by saying fear; however, fear (and stress) are not thoughts, but emotions. The amygdala first associates the fire alarm with some kind of danger and puts us in action mode to flee the danger. I then ask, "If during the presentation in view behind me on the stage is a firefighter working on the fire alarm and it goes off, what would your thoughts be?" Many respond "not to worry; it's not real." Once again, in just nanoseconds, a previously held thought pattern associating someone working on an alarm with the sounds of a fire alarm triggers our emotion (relief). We have many previously held thought patterns that make us successful and productive. However, we also have some that jeopardize our rational decision-making responses and emotional well being. This is why it is important to become skilled at using the strategies presented in Chapter 6, so as not to fall victim to a previously held nonproductive thought.

I can recall my first year as principal leading my very first professional development session. I had spent hours and hours preparing for the daylong event—and even rented a country club so we could go off-site. During a work session I placed teachers in teams. One teacher, for whom I now have the utmost respect, started loudly expressing how upset she was with the day's proceedings. Maybe she felt the day was not planned well. Maybe she felt I was insensitive in how I grouped the teachers. Whatever the cause, her reaction caught me off guard. Fortunately, I had been reading Good to Great (Collins, 2001) and knew that some great companies have tense and argumentative meetings. I needed to maintain my composure no matter how much my stomach was churning inside. I wanted to sneak off to a corner of the room and hide! I told her that I was disappointed with how she felt about the day and tried to learn more about her feelings.

When I followed up with the teacher a few days later, she shared that she had come to the new school to be part of a schoolwide team, but she felt that as a physical education (non-academic) teacher, she was excluded from teaming. After hearing this, I told her that, had I been in her shoes, I probably would have been equally angry. However, I gave her some strategies on how she could have managed her emotions and explained the importance of team members' being responsible to each other. If I would not have followed up with her and had carried around a grudge for weeks, this would not only have affected the working relationship between the teacher and me, but also would have made the entire staff uncomfortable. Following up when people get their feelings hurt is important whether the action was intentional or not.

Identifying possible triggers

One of the best strategies for controlling your emotions is to identify possible "triggers" that could cause you to become emotionally hijacked. Triggers may be behaviors, language, people, or events that evoke an emotion. Based on a past experience, a traumatic incident, or a bad relationship, triggers likely cause a "fight or flight" response. If you know ahead of time what your triggers are, you can be prepared to practice another emotionally intelligent strategy and control your emotions. Even though your amygdala may once again sacrifice accuracy for speed, you will have already recognized that the perceived threat is not a real threat. You may now pause, presume positive intentions, use Stop-Look-Listen or other strategies, and successfully control your emotions. When I do workshops for schools or leadership preparation programs, in one activity each participant is asked to identify three of his or her own triggers. Most frequently, group members' triggers are phone calls from parents, calls from the central office, a particular teacher openly questioning a decision, someone showing up late for a meeting, and attendees not paying attention in meetings.

Case study: E-mail triggers anger. One of the more interesting coaching sessions came after Chip told about receiving an e-mail from a board member who had heard a rumor at church. Chip became very upset at the questions the board member asked and sent a negative reply back. Chip had forwarded me the e-mail as soon as he sent the reply. I immediately called him because I knew the response he sent was out of character. Chip had said that he tried to call me during the day for advice, but instead of waiting to send the e-mail, he went ahead and sent it. Chip wrote in his journal about the incident:

> I became angry and scared when I got the e-mail. I am tired of being underappreciated and second-guessed by people. I let my emotions control my actions; and I sent a negative e-mail, escalating the situation. I could have stopped and recognized how I was feeling and thought a little more based on those feelings. Then I could have decided how I should respond to the e-mail, or if I should have responded at all immediately. Obviously, I did not do that; I don't know why. I know I made it worse and knew that when I did it. This was self-destructive behavior and something that's not like me.

Explaining his thoughts and the feelings immediately after receiving the e-mail, Chip said,

> I was angry and scared. I was scared because of the negative rumors that are out there; if the levy does not pass, I could lose my position. I want to do a good job, and all we hear is negative, negative, negative. I pride myself on doing a good job, and I do not need people to stroke me and praise me; but when you constantly hear how things are messed up, you start to wonder, what do people really think of the job I am doing?

Asked whether he was aware of any other thoughts as he expressed his emotions, Chip went on to add:

> My first thought was, Should board members be sending me e-mails like this? Should it have been sent to me and copied to all board members and the superintendent? If there is really a question about this situation, why not just e-mail me? I think the board member was asking the questions for the wrong reasons.

Chip explained he was upset not because the e-mail was inappropriate, but because it was copied to all the other board members. Trying to create a positive intention hypothesis, I asked whether there might have been a conscious effort by principals and board members to keep everyone informed of any comments or concerns because election day for the upcoming levy was near. Because Chip dealt with many people who were upset or unhappy, he had to create a new mental model to improve his emotional intelligence. This new mental model would trigger emotions when he received e-mails that he was unsure about.

Chip realizes the board members' present perception of his ability to handle conflict is negative and says of similar situations in the future: "I know there are different options. I know next time not to react. I will not respond immediately." In his journal Chip wrote, "I should have thought how the person who sent the e-mail felt. I should have addressed her concerns without becoming defensive and angry. What I did was counterproductive. I felt very nervous about apologizing to the board member later. I explained to her that I understood how she felt and explained why I responded so poorly to her e-mail."

After reading Chip's case study, reflect about how you would have handled the situation in an emotionally intelligent manner. You could have used the strategy of pausing and not responding so quickly to the upsetting e-mail or the strategy "What would I suggest to a colleague?" The challenge for Chip throughout our emotional intelligence training was getting rid of previously held, nonproductive thought patterns and really focusing on the positive intentions of others.

Case study: Handling triggers and improving leadership. Interestingly, almost six weeks later, Chip faced a similar situation. Because the athletic field was too wet for play, he had to cancel a soccer tournament game. The soccer coach, many players, and parents assumed the game had been cancelled in order to preserve the field for a Friday night football game. A parent and a board member who was a parent e-mailed Chip questioning his decision and citing rumors they had heard about "the football coach canceling the soccer game." Chip called me and forwarded me the e-mails. Although not pleased by the e-mails, Chip recognized that e-mails from parents were one of his triggers, so he immediately paused and started thinking about what emotional intelligence strategy he could use. He chose to presume positive intentions, which gave him perspective about why the e-mails had been sent.

Practicing his emotional intelligence strategies, he sent a return e-mail to the parents thanking them for coming to him for accurate information, and he explained the situation. He also empathized with them about the cancellation of the game and shared his excitement for the boys' soccer team's success and the opportunity to host a soccer game. When Chip forwarded a copy of his response to me, he attached a positive note stating he was improving his emotional intelligence. Because Chip is aware that e-mails from possibly upset parents are a trigger for him, he can now do a better job of controlling his emotions, which will result in improved leadership. Regardless of your triggers, you will be a more effective leader if you identify them before you are surprised in the workplace.

Case study: Presumed negative intentions as trigger. When asked permission by a teacher to take her yearly evaluation home to read, one school leader thought, "What is this about? Is she going to contest the evaluation and not sign it?" The principal thought,

> I almost took the request as an indication she did not trust me. This is something I really need to work on. I don't know how you get past this, assuming you know what teachers are thinking or what their motives are. I assumed the reason that she wanted to read this further is because she really doesn't trust the administration and that I might have unfairly put something bad in there.

The principal shared that although the teacher's evaluation was positive, he worried all night about possible negative outcomes.

Case study: Question yourself and ask for proof. When a teacher took the initiative to ask the central office for support for a project that she and her principal were working on together, the principal thought this reflected negatively on him. The school leader explained,

I felt a teacher went over my head during a recent event. It turned out to be a huge miscommunication. When the teacher asked me a question, I responded that we would have to find out. She went ahead and checked out the situation, and I thought that made me look bad. It makes me look like I am not working hard or following through. When I tell somebody I am going to do something, I will. This is one of my strengths. I think it is disrespectful to go around someone.

When asked whether this teacher or any of his teachers would do anything intentionally to make him look bad, the school leader immediately looked relieved and answered with a rhetorical question, "No, so why should I get upset?" By just pausing and using the strategies "Question yourself and ask for proof" and "Presume positive intentions," the principal could have managed his emotions better.

Case study: Confrontation triggers defensiveness. During an administrative meeting a teacher confronted a building principal about a comment he allegedly had made that created a major problem for another staff member. Becoming very defensive, the principal lashed out at the teacher for believing secondhand information. The principal shared in a coaching session:

> I never stopped for one moment and thought how the teacher may have been feeling. I know now that she was extremely upset at the situation and because of my defensiveness, I communicated unintentionally that I am more concerned with my own feelings than hers.

The principal really lost a golden opportunity to demonstrate empathy for the teacher and openness and transparency with his staff. If the principal could have paused and recognized what triggered his defensiveness, he might have realized how difficult it must have been for the teacher to confront him, expressed his appreciation for her going to the source, and stated his position without attacking her. The emphasis would have centered more on listening and trying to understand what the teacher was thinking and feeling than on his own anger.

Regardless of the strategy that you choose to use to help yourself control your emotions, it is important to have some strategies in your toolbox. You will confront many emotional experiences in your position, so developing a repertoire of "self-control" skills is important to your effectiveness as a leader.

➡ Steps to improve your emotional self-control

1. Record incidents from the last year to which you reacted negatively and ones to which you responded appropriately. Identify what triggered both the positive and negative behaviors. For the positive responses, what helped you respond appropriately? Were the triggers for negative reactions different from the triggers for positive responses?

2. Practice pausing and identifying your feelings during intense situations. Record these "practices" in your journal. Notice your learning curve: is it a smooth straight upward curve, or are there dips in it as you learn more about the nuances of improving your self control?

3. Identify all of your triggers that evoke negative emotions. Beside each trigger, identify a strategy that you would like to practice when the trigger happens.

Chapter 9
Goals and Emotional Intelligence

I have not really been sensitive to everyone else. This has been the biggest change I have been trying to make. I want to continue to improve in this area as well as make myself even more approachable for my staff.

—Rick, School Principal

One of the most efficient methods of learning how to develop leadership skills is by working with a coach. Hopefully, this book's emotional intelligence assessments, strategies for improving emotional intelligence, and case studies have helped you understand the importance and benefits of coaching. As your own coach, you must realize the importance of the goal setting that occurs after reviewing your Self and Staff Rater Assessments. Chapter 9 discusses the process of working on goals and the steps involved in your journey to improve your leadership capabilities.

The focus of the chapter is a case study about Rick, a principal who completed his emotional intelligence training a few years ago. Although at the time there were many challenges and setbacks, Rick also made significant improvements. Today, Rick is enjoying more success, better relationships, and a healthier life. The case study explores his goal setting based on his emotional intelligence assessment and coaching session transcripts. Answering questions throughout the chapter will give you practice choosing appropriate strategies.

Rick's challenges and solutions

Before taking an emotional intelligence assessment, Rick identified these challenges of his job.

Challenge #1: Rick had always been an ambitious person, and this combined with his competitiveness and extreme sensitivity often created leadership challenges and stress for him. Rick wants to win any and all debates or discussions. During problem-solving opportunities or meetings when people openly share ideas, he wants his ideas to be chosen.

Solution: A great starting point for Rick was to balance inquiry and advocacy. Always an advocate for his opinions, insights and ideas, Rick seldom takes the opportunity to explore others' ideas and opinions. As the leader he should facilitate conversations and collaborative efforts to get as many great ideas and as much information as possible upon which to base his decisions. Instead of using meeting time trying to persuade others to see his point of view, Rick's focus should center on listening and understanding others' points of view. Before every meeting and collaborative opportunity, Rick reminded himself to ask for others' ideas and emotions.

Challenge #2: Because Rick was easily frustrated when people needed the time to process his ideas or did not agree with him, staff members quickly learned that if you disagreed with Rick, you would have to debate him (and he would not like losing).

Solution: Rick agreed that when people are hearing an idea for the first time, they need time to process and reflect upon it. Rick and I discussed his personality of being a "risk-taker" and his lack of fearing failure. I suggested he use professional development activities that would highlight personality differences among the administrators and faculty and show that the more diversity in the group, the greater opportunity for a wide range of input. Rick began to see himself as a coach preparing his teachers for a marathon they would all run. If everyone was at the starting line with him and willing to cover the same course, it would not matter whether people walked, skipped and/or ran to the finish or what their times would be. Given individual differences, there would likely be staff requiring patience and support from their leader to even develop the confidence to run the marathon.

Challenge #3: Perceived by others as overly confident, Rick was basically insecure. Although quick to be direct and honest with others, he was defensive when people gave him direct, honest feedback. During any times of disagreement, Rick was emotionally hijacked resulting in poor, aggressive reactions to others.

While self confidence and a strong ego have been characteristics of effective leaders, they have also been the demise of many leaders (Collins, 2002). It was Collins' "Level Five Leadership" that called for a balance between humility and ego. In discussing his behaviors that led others to view him as overly confident, Rick acknowledged that he seldom was without an answer, opinion, or idea—no matter what the subject. Rick shared in an interview:

I was successful at a relatively early age in life and so with that developed confidence came an "I know how to do it attitude." I think it stems back from when I became a school principal at 28 … and I know that comes across.

Solution: Rick's focus was to empower his staff to act and to avoid micromanaging. By empowering people to act and offering his support of their actions, his staff would develop the autonomy and confidence to be fully functional. Empowering and supporting his staff would mean that Rick would have to learn to listen more, ask more questions, and acknowledge the validity of solutions other than his during problem-solving sessions.

Following his request for my help with solutions to some problems at his school, he had become defensive when I suggested alternatives to the ones he had tried previously. Both his body language and tone of voice had changed from the time he asked for help and the time he heard the answer. He needed to learn that others' ideas, opinions, and suggestions were not personal judgments about him, they were just alternatives. And likewise, if he learned not to harshly judge his staff, but to empower them, develop their self confidence, and ask more questions than give answers, Rick could change others' perceptions of him.

Emotional intelligence assessment and goals

After completing the emotional intelligence assessment, we established specific goals that would enable Rick to effectively implement the solutions discussed earlier. Like many other principals, Rick was really surprised and disappointed with some of his scores on his emotional intelligence assessment. As I remind everyone, view the feedback as a gift.

Rick identified three major goals for his emotional intelligence development.

A. Emotional Self-Management;

B. Emotional Self-Expression; and

C. Emotional Self-Control.

Communicating hope. During times of change in our schools, we identify our hopes to gain our staff's commitment to the change process. Likewise, it was important for Rick to identify what he hoped for at the end of his journey. Rick decided to measure his success in meeting his goals by having better relationships with others, less stress, and more job and life satisfaction. You too, should write down what your hopes are for completing the emotional intelligence training in this book. How will you feel? How will your relationships change? What will your school look like?

Working on goals. Important to working on goals is dedicating time for reflection and journaling. At the end of this chapter are charts you may use, or perhaps you will create your own forms for recording your thoughts, feelings, and behaviors as opportunities arise for improving your emotional intelligence; this is just as important as writing your goals.

For the three months I coached Rick while he worked on his goals, we began each session by setting the day's agenda. During each session we explored Rick's recollections of any of the week's situations or events related to any of the dimensions in his Genos Assessment. Over the duration of the coaching sessions, Rick had many opportunities to practice his new skills. Rick handled some situations well, and he struggled with others. I encouraged Rick to learn the most from all that he was experiencing by fully reflecting about those experiences. The challenge with emotional intelligence is that you can concentrate on displaying proper emotions and behaviors over several months and yet in one moment, if you allow yourself to become hijacked, you can threaten relationships you had worked hard to develop.

For some of the skills of this program to become a habit, you will need to practice them for at least two months. You may decide to reflect, work on your journal, and keep track of your goals daily or once a week. Whatever you decide, establish a regular routine of your emotional intelligence work. Try to be very specific in recording exactly what you were thinking and feeling and how you behaved. Also include a few comments about whether or not you achieved the desire outcome and what you would do differently next time.

Rick's first goal. Rick's first goal was to be in more control of his emotions, which is in the area of Emotional Self-Management. During one of our earlier coaching sessions Rick told of his frustration at justifying a decision for a faculty member three times within the course of a few days. Later in the day after his third explanation of the decision, an uninvolved teacher asked for information about the decision. As we talked after the situation, Rick said, "I should have just focused on the fact that this teacher had no information about the earlier conversations and was just trying to help. Instead I over-reacted and ended up having to apologize."

Rick and I discussed the importance of Emotional Self-Control. Although he may have not have displayed anger toward the first teacher, he certainly must have been feeling anger, which he carried around with him until he reacted poorly to someone else. As very busy school leaders, I pointed out to Rick, when we have to use our precious time to correct mistakes that we continue to make, we are less productive and our school suffers. As Rick's coach, what strategies would you suggest for him to improve his Emotional Self-Management and Emotional Self-Control?

Rick's second goal. Rick's second goal was improving his Emotional Expression, the area in which his staff rated him lowest on their assessments. Rick often communicated that he was upset through e-mails or notes. Highly expressive in writing his thoughts and feelings in his journal, he felt he could express himself better in writing than in person. Although writing positive notes is an excellent strategy for creating a positive culture, using e-mail or writing notes to handle conflict is a poor choice because it is impossible to view and manage the emotions of the reader.

Case Study: Sandy, the staff planning chair, e-mailed Rick that the agenda of a meeting he had planned but now was unable to attend was going to change. Frustrated by the change in his agenda, Rick e-mailed a reply to Sandy expressing his displeasure. Rick went on to explain:

> I thought about not sending the e-mail, but then I wanted to see how she would respond. Indeed, she responded nastily. So I e-mailed that we needed to meet. She said she was too busy to meet, but I insisted we meet as soon as possible.

During the meeting, she became defensive and started crying. Before reading further, take a moment to consider what suggestions you have for Rick. What are some strategies for helping him develop Emotional Expression? Assess the impact of using e-mail for expressing emotions.

Our analysis of the situation resulted in two main points. Presuming positive intentions might have led to his considering that the teacher might not feel comfortable leading a meeting in which the agenda was set by someone who would not be present. She may have feared that she would not produce a result that would satisfy him. If Rick had tried to understand what the teacher was feeling and thinking, he might not have reacted so poorly.

The other point involved Rick's major goal of improving his emotional expression by becoming aware of when his body language and tone of voice intimidated his staff. In an attempt to hide his lack of ability in handling conflict, Rick addressed some intense, emotional situations by e-mail. Recall from Chapter 5 that we get lots of emotional information from interacting with others that can help us make better decisions. If you are communicating via e-mail, how do you know what the other person is thinking or feeling? What are their body language and facial expressions telling you as they read your message? Although retreating to an office to e-mail some tough questions or direct statements is easier than facing someone with those remarks, you lose an opportunity to collect valuable emotional information. In addition, you can never be sure that someone reads your e-mail in the same context as it was written. Many times Rick turned to e-mail not only because he felt uncomfortable expressing his emotions, but also because it turned out to be a byproduct of his first goal, Emotional Self-Management. When Rick was frustrated or angry, he would turn to one of his strengths and write his thoughts and emotions. Although reflecting in an electronic journal is not a bad strategy for learning to manage emotions, it is not at all appropriate to send e-mail reflections. Almost every two weeks during his three months of coaching, Rick struggled with this weakness of expressing his emotions about a conflict via e-mail. However, by the time of the program's conclusion, Rick was able, after starting to e-mail someone, to stop and go speak directly with the person.

Rick's third goal. Ricks third goal was improving his Emotional Self-Control. During one session, Rick was very frustrated after one of his most disappointing days ever. Committed to leading his building on the journey of becoming a professional learning community, Rick thought his staff had taken a step backward that day; actually, the expression on his face made me think it had been more than a step, but a stampede. Rick explained that over the year his faculty had been spending its professional development on writing short cycle assessments and common assessments. Part of this process was reviewing the progress reports that were sent home to parents. Just after the students' progress reports had been sent home, he realized that a whole grade level had failed to follow through using the correct process. Instead of reporting each student's progress, the teachers collectively just copied into the report all of the indicators that were covered. Rick shared his frustration.

> The whole 4th grade team decided that this was too much work. … So each progress report almost looked identical! When I notified them by e-mail that we needed to talk because they did not follow the expectations, they came to my office and ganged up on me. Two teachers said they did not understand what was expected, and another said it was just too much work and made several personal and unprofessional comments. I sent the one teacher who made the unprofessional and personal comments another e-mail.

If you were Rick's coach what would be some of the first questions you would ask Rick? What strategies would you reinforce?

My coaching strategy was to first review presuming positive intentions, which might have resulted in the assumption that the teachers had made an honest mistake and unintentionally had not followed the grading process. My second strategy was questioning the use of e-mail. And, finally I asked Rick whether when communicating his expectations and disappointment, he had tried to understand what it would feel like to be one of the teachers receiving it.

A principal with high emotional intelligence would have gone directly to the teachers in a nonthreatening manner and asked about the grades to gather the facts. During this time the principal would be empathetic and try to understand what, if any, emotions the staff may have been feeling. After all, being questioned by your principal about grades is an automatically fear-inducing incident, and presumably, the teachers had good intentions. A principal with high emotional intelligence would then choose whether or not to express emotions. If the principal chose not to, then he or she should be able to function the rest of the day without any bottled-up emotions. Finally, a principal high in emotional intelligence would probably have asked if there were any solutions to resolve the situation for parents and students, and what could be done to avoid this situation occurring in the future.

➡️ Goal setting

1. Use the following goal sheet to identify two or three goals to improve your emotional intelligence. Choose the dimensions you feel have the greatest opportunity for development after reviewing your emotional intelligence assessments.

Skill	Goals for the Week
Emotional Self-Awareness	
Emotional Expression	
Emotional Awareness of Others	
Emotional Reasoning	
Emotional Self-Management	
Emotional Management of Others	
Emotional Self-Control	

2. Use the Success Sheet to record when you successfully used your emotional intelligence in any appropriate dimension.

Skill	Successes Experienced Last Week
Emotional Self-Awareness	
Emotional Expression	
Emotional Awareness of Others	
Emotional Reasoning	
Emotional Self-Management	
Emotional Management of Others	
Emotional Self-Control	

Chapter 10

In Their Own Words: Three Principals and EI

This has totally changed my thinking about how to deal with emotions rather than just setting them aside. I now can dive into them [emotions] and deal with them. It's not that I did not care, I thought it was irrelevant. —School Leader

As mentioned earlier, some of the case studies in this book were from the experiences of real school leaders, while others were fictional. At this point of the book, you likely have a solid understanding of emotional intelligence, have reviewed your emotional intelligence assessment, and have identified goals for your professional development. During the next several months review your goals daily or weekly, and reflect on all interpersonal interactions in which emotional information was available. Did you handle yourself well? Did you respond appropriately? Did you over react? What strategies seemed to work best for you in controlling and managing your emotions? Committing to this process will be challenging and filled with successes and setbacks. During this chapter we will review some of the feedback, analyses, and reflections of other school administrators who went through an emotional intelligence training and coaching program. Hopefully, the words and progress of fellow school leaders will inspire you to commit to your own developmental program.

During a focus group discussion, I asked three school leaders what were the most common emotions that each experienced most frequently as principals. All three administrators reported, "Happiness." This was quite shocking to me, especially after spending so many hours of coaching and listening to the challenges that each of them faced. But I came to realize that this happiness was what kept each school leader focused on what sometimes feels to them like an insurmountable task of educating all their students. Remember this often: you are in this challenging job because you love what you do. Next, I asked the three school leaders what emotions challenged them the most in their positions. Paula answered, "Fear," Chip answered, "Fear and anger," and Rick answered, "Anger."

The importance of emotional intelligence

During three months of coaching, interviews, and focus groups, three school leaders all shared similar sentiments.

Paula, who had spent the last four years completing her doctorate in education, stated that she thought that developing and using emotional intelligence may be the most important task in school administration. She said:

> I think it might be the most important skill of a school leader. I think to lead you have to know where teachers are emotionally. Book knowledge, research, and all that can be taught to people, but the process of emotional intelligence, of knowing yourself and others, is much more important.

Paula also entered in her journal how being aware of her feelings and thoughts influenced her decisions:

> Your frame of mind influences your approach to daily decisions. For example when I am already frustrated, I am more predisposed to make quick, reactive decisions as opposed to patient, thoughtful ones.

Rick agreed about the importance of emotional intelligence and understanding your own emotions. He shared:

> If you are going to lead people you must understand people. The more you can understand them and what they bring to the table, the better you can lead them. This makes you aware of the need to deal with people differently. One size does not fit all.

> I have always believed I was a sensitive person, I mean I could get my feelings hurt. But I have not really been sensitive to everyone else. This has been the biggest change I have been trying to make. I want to continue to improve in this area as well as make myself even more approachable for my staff.

Chip, too, had strong opinions about the importance of high emotional intelligence for school leaders. In a final interview he said,

> Logic and reason as great as they are, [they] are not the end all. Unless you deal with how people feel about things, logic and reasoning do not matter. No one is going to buy into what you are leading unless you get past their fears or

emotions. I have always been a very logical and reasoning person, and that is not enough. I always thought it was, but it is not. It is incredibly important to recognize your own emotions because you have to deal with those emotions before you can communicate with anyone else. You don't want to be hijacked. You also want to understand others' emotions so you can try to understand where they are coming from and why they have a concern or issue. If you need to lead change you need to address how people are feeling and not just what they are thinking. To help get people where they need to be, you must understand emotional intelligence.

Rick, Chip, and Paula all reported that becoming more emotionally intelligent is an important objective in their positions. I asked each school leader, "What percentage of the challenges you have faced this year have required you to rely on emotional intelligence?" They had similar responses. Paula answered, "80%; it is a people business. I have used it with kids, parents and staff." Rick stated that 100% of his responsibilities have to do with his using emotional intelligence. Chip stated that 100% of his assistant principal role involved using emotional intelligence skills. During interviews at the midpoint and at the end of the coaching sessions Rick, Chip, and Paula were asked open-ended questions regarding the benefits of understanding emotional intelligence. Each responded favorably. Paula said,

> I think this has made realize more than ever to seek input and opinions continually. It has made me more effective in the way I think about things, and has given me some perspective. It has helped me be more patient about making decisions and about how other people make their decisions. I get less frustrated. It is still too early to tell whether I am a more effective leader or not, but I am less frustrated.

In a focus group discussion Paula also shared, "My awareness for others' emotions has been heightened. I used to solicit some thoughts and opinions from others, but now I am more aware of their emotions."

Paula also added in an interview at the conclusion of the program:

> One of the things I really focus on now is having the same relationships and doing the things I do with managers and peers as I do with my direct reports. My direct reports' scores were much better. I listened more, supported more, and tried to understand more with my direct reports than I did my peers and mangers. Now I consciously try to use some of the tools that have been successful with direct reports with my managers and peers.

If you like, you, too, could have your teachers, peers, and supervisors complete the emotional intelligence instrument to get feedback about how you display emotional intelligence and compare the difference in scores between your staff and your self assessments. Sometimes getting a variety of views is very insightful. The research suggests that people tend to overrate themselves and that direct report ratings (teacher ratings) are more closely related to actual job performance.

Through her efforts in improving her emotional intelligence, Paula now believes she will be more effective. Mirroring Paula's remarks, Chip's response about the benefits of the emotional intelligence program was:

> It has made me more effective in dealing with people and recognizing what I am doing. I am also better at recognizing why people do what they are doing. It has been helpful in talking to our adults in the building as well as our kids. I probably have said this 100 times, there are a lot of things I have never thought of before; I would do things by reacting to them or on impulse. Now I don't have those reactions as often; I think about what a person may mean as well as what they have said. I know this has been very beneficial and successful regardless of the post assessments.

Once again, if you are interested in evaluating how much you have improved after six months, ask the same people that initially rated your emotional intelligence to complete the staff assessment tool again while you do another self- assessment. Compare the differences.

At the midway point, Rick reported the benefits of the emotional intelligence coaching program:

> This forces you to take time to reflect and think about how you respond to people and emotions. I think we all make mistakes, and sometimes say, "I won't do it this way next time." Next time comes, and you do it the exact same way. But if you take the coaching seriously, practice your skills and do some thinking in the down time, you can avoid those bad mistakes when the events occur. When you are about to get hijacked, you can respond differently because of all the time you spent reflecting.

Paula shared these comments during her last interview:

> My perspective on things has definitely changed a lot. I think it is easier now to handle certain situations that won't eat at me. "This is how people react, it's valid. Now, what are our choices?" It helps stabilize you more. This gives you perspective on how to deal with people. As a leader this is more beneficial

than even knowing the latest research on a topic. It's more beneficial because you can get more out of your staff, students, and yourself.

I totally changed my assumptions about how other people feel. I never considered it before. It's not that I did not care; I thought it was irrelevant. I concentrated more on showing and telling people how I felt.

Start today

By now you understand what emotional intelligence is, how improving your emotional intelligence will improve your leadership skills, how different school leaders have used emotional intelligence strategies to lead schools, how to prevent emotional hijacking, and what your triggers are. You also have the Genos Assessment Results and a development plan as a map for your journey to success and fulfillment.

After a school year of working hard on your emotional intelligence skills, your next step may be to participate in an Emotional Intelligence 360-Degree Assessment. This assessment will give you anonymous feedback from your staff, peers, and supervisors on their perceptions of your emotional intelligence. You can contact Genos at www.genosamericas.com or contact the author at www.inspiremyschool.com.

An important part of your journey is to be patient with your progress. Learning to change your behavior will take time and practice. Good luck on your new journey, and thank you for your commitment to serve. Remember, you do have one of the most important jobs in the world. Without your leadership, our children will never reach their fullest potential.

Appendix A
Genos Emotional Intelligence Inventory
Self-Assessment (Concise)

Instructions

The Genos Emotional Intelligence Inventory measures how often you believe you demonstrate emotionally intelligent behaviors at work. There are no right or wrong answers. However, it is essential that your responses truly reflect your beliefs regarding how often you demonstrate the behavior in question. You should not answer in a way that you think sounds good or acceptable. In general try not to spend too long thinking about responses. Most often the first answer that occurs to you is the most accurate. However, do not rush your responses or respond without giving due consideration to each statement.

Read each statement on the next page (100) about a behavior and indicate on the response scale how often you believe you demonstrate the behavior in question. Circle the number that corresponds to your answer.

When considering a response it is important not to think of the way you behaved in any one situation, rather your responses should be based on your typical behavior. If a question does not give you as much information as you think you need, choose a response that seems most likely. Although there is no time limit, it should take about 5 minutes to complete.

	Almost Never	Seldom	Sometimes	Usually	Almost Always
1. I appropriately communicate decisions to staff and parents.	1	2	3	4	5
2. I fail to recognize how my feelings drive my behavior at work.	1	2	3	4	5
3. When upset at work, I still think clearly.	1	2	3	4	5
4. I fail to handle stressful situations at work effectively.	1	2	3	4	5
5. I understand the things that make people feel optimistic at work.	1	2	3	4	5
6. I fail to keep calm in difficult situations at work.	1	2	3	4	5
7. I am effective in helping others feel positive at work.	1	2	3	4	5
8. I find it difficult to identify the things that motivate people at work.	1	2	3	4	5
9. I consider the way others may react to decisions when communicating them.	1	2	3	4	5
10. I have trouble finding the right words to express how I feel at work.	1	2	3	4	5
11. When I get frustrated with something at work I discuss my frustration appropriately.	1	2	3	4	5
12. I don't know what to do or say when the staff get upset at work.	1	2	3	4	5
13. I am aware of my mood state at work.	1	2	3	4	5
14. I effectively deal with things that annoy me at work.	1	2	3	4	5

Scoring

To score your assessment results:

1. Add the response numbers you circled for questions 1, 3, 5, 7, 9, 11, 13 and 14. For example if you circled 3 for question 1; 4 for question 3; 1 for question 5 then you would add 3+4+1 for a total of 8. The total score for odd-numbered answers and the answer to question 14 is _____.
2. Put the numbers of the responses you circled for questions 2, 4, 6, 8, 10, 12 in the second column (labelled "number you circled") in the table below.

Question number	Number you circled	New number
2		
4		
6		
8		
10		
12		

Total even answers:_____

3. Fill in the column above called "new number" by using the conversion table below.

Number you circled	New number
1	5
2	4
3	3
4	2
5	1

4. Add the total numbers for the even questions in the table at the top of the page. The total of the even-numbered answers is _____.

5. Add the total numbers calculated at step 1 and step 4. The total for all answers is _____. Use the table below to understand your score.

If you scored yourself between	Description: Then you believe that you...
14–27	Demonstrate very little emotionally intelligent behavior at work. Ask yourself what has led you to this conclusion? What happens to you and your colleagues as a result? Would a high score be beneficial to you?
28–41	Demonstrate some emotionally intelligent behavior at work.
42–55	Demonstrate a considerable amount of emotionally intelligent behavior at work. Where are your strengths? Where can you improve?
56–70	Demonstrate emotionally intelligent workplace behaviors very often in your work. Ask yourself "what would others say?" What happens to you and your colleagues as a result? Can you develop this behavior in others? Does this high focus on being emotionally intelligent in your behavior at work come at a cost to other areas?

Appendix B
Genos Staff Rater EI Assessment (Concise)

Name of Leader:_____

Instructions

This survey is designed to measure how often you believe the person named above demonstrates emotionally intelligent behaviors at work. There are no right or wrong answers. The person above is committed to soliciting accurate, anonymous feedback for his or her own professional and personal development. Do not put your name on the paper. It is essential that your responses truly reflect your beliefs regarding how often you feel the person demonstrates the behaviors in question. You should not answer in a way that you think sounds good or acceptable. In general try not to spend too long thinking about responses. Most often the first answer that occurs to you is the most accurate. However, do not rush your responses or respond without giving due consideration to each statement.

Read each statement on the next page (104) about a behavior and circle on the response scale how often the leader above demonstrates the behavior.

When considering a response, base your answer on typical behavior patterns and not on the behavior in any one situation. Also, if a question does not give all the information you need, choose a response that seems most likely. Although there is no time limit, it should take about 5 minutes to complete. When you have completed the assessment, please return it to:

_____

	Almost Never	Seldom	Sometimes	Usually	Almost Always
1. He or she appropriately communicates his or her decisions to the staff and parents.	1	2	3	4	5
2. He or she fails to recognize how his or her feelings drive his or her behavior at work.	1	2	3	4	5
3. When upset at work, he or she still thinks clearly.	1	2	3	4	5
4. He or she fails to handle stressful situations at work effectively.	1	2	3	4	5
5. He or she understands the things that make people feel optimistic at work.	1	2	3	4	5
6. He or she fails to keep calm in difficult situations at work.	1	2	3	4	5
7. He or she is effective in helping others feel positive at work.	1	2	3	4	5
8. He or she finds it difficult to identify the things that motivate people at work.	1	2	3	4	5
9. He or she considers the way others may react to decisions when communicating them.	1	2	3	4	5
10. He or she has trouble finding the right words to express how he or she feels at work.	1	2	3	4	5
11. When he or she gets frustrated with something at work, he/she discusses his or her frustrations appropriately.	1	2	3	4	5
12. He or she does not know what to do or say when the staff gets upset at work.	1	2	3	4	5
13. He or she is aware of his or her mood while at work.	1	2	3	4	5
14. He or she effectively deals with things that annoy him or her at work.	1	2	3	4	5

Appendix C
Scoring the Staff Assessment

To score your assessment use the table on the next page (20 staff members) or create your own with a row for every staff member and a column for every question.

1. Record and add the response numbers the staff circled for questions 1, 3, 5, 7, 9, 11, 13, and 14, and divide by the number of scores to get an average score.

2. Record and **reverse the response numbers** your staff circled for questions 2, 4, 6, 8, 10, 12 using the table below and then add them as per step 1.

Old number	New number
1	5
2	4
3	3
4	2
5	1

	#1	#2	#3	#4	#5	#6	#7	#8	#9	#10	#11	#12	#13	#14
1														
2														
3														
4														
5														
6														
7														
8														
9														
10														
11														
12														
13														
14														
15														
16														
17														
18														
19														
20														
Total														
Ave.														

3. Add the total numbers calculated at step 1 and step 2. Average the score for each question and add to get an overall total score. Use the table below to understand your score.

If your staff scored you between	Description: Then they believe that you…
14–27	Demonstrate very little emotionally intelligent behavior at work. Think about what may have led them to this conclusion. What might happen as a result of this when you interact with your colleagues? What benefits might a high score bring to your leadership?
28–41	Demonstrate some emotionally intelligent behavior at work.
42–55	Demonstrate a considerable amount of emotionally intelligent behavior at work. What would they say are your strengths? Things you can improve?
56–70	Demonstrate emotionally intelligent workplace behaviors very often in your work. What happens to you and your colleagues as a result? Can you develop this behavior in others? Does this high focus on being emotionally intelligent in your behavior at work come at a cost to other areas?

Appendix D
Examining the Gaps Between Self-Assessment and Staff Assessment Scores

Remember, most people become defensive and go through a grieving process when examining the scores of others for the first time. Your staff has cared enough about you as a person and your commitment to professional and personal development that they have given you some accurate and beneficial feedback. Despite the fact that some staff members may have scored you much lower than other staff members in certain areas, focus on your average scores. Leaders who have tried to identify raters who scored them lower in certain areas or communicated to staff members that they were disappointed in some of the scores have jeopardized their leadership as well as trust and honesty in the work place. You have asked for honest and direct feedback; now use this information to begin your journey of self development. Follow the directions on the next page (108) to examine the gaps in your self-assessment and staff assessment scores.

Ratings														
1														
2														
3														
4														
5														
Question #	1	2	3	4	5	6	7	8	9	10	11	12	13	14
Dimension	ER	ESA	ESC	ESM	EAO	ESC	EMO	EAO	ER	EE	EE	EMO	ESA	ESM

GENOS Emotional Intelligence Dimension abbreviations in the chart are:

ESA–Emotional Self-Awareness,

EE–Emotional Expression,

EAO–Emotional Awareness of Others,

ER–Emotional Reasoning

ESM–Emotional Self-Management,

EMO–Emotional Management of Others,

ESM–Emotional Self-Control.

For a definition and description of workplace outcomes of each dimension, see Figure 1 p. 9.

Staff Scores: Using a red pen, plot the average score for each question from Appendix C (p. 105). Look at your lower scores. To which emotional intelligence dimensions from Figure 1 (p. 9) did each question refer? Is there a pattern in your stronger scores? What dimensions did you do better in? Is there a pattern in your lower scores? What dimensions were they in?

Self Scores: Using a blue or black pen, plot your scores for each question from Appendix A (p. 99). What areas did you rate yourself higher in than your staff? Why are their perceptions different than yours? What effect does this have on your school? What areas did you and your staff score similarly?

References

Ashkanasy, N. M., & Daus, C. S. (2005). Rumors of the death of emotional intelligence in organizational behavior are vastly exaggerated. *Journal of Organizational Behavior, 26,* 441–452.

Ashton, P. T., & Webb, R. B. (1986). *Making a difference: Teachers' sense of efficacy and student achievement.* White Plains, NY: Longman.

Bar-On, R. (1997). *Emotional quotient inventory (EQ-i): Technical manual.* Toronto, ON: Multi-Health Systems.

Barling, J., Slater, F., & Kelloway, E. K. (2000). Transformational leadership and emotional intelligence: An exploratory study. *Leadership & Organization Development Journal, 21*(3), 157–161.

Bass, B. M., & Yammarino, F. J. (1991). Congruence of self and others' leadership ratings of naval officers for understanding successful performance. *Applied Psychology: An International Review, 40,* 437–454.

Blankenstein, A. M. (2004). *Failure is not an option: Six principles that guide student achievement in high performing schools.* Thousand Oaks, CA; Corwin Press.

Bredeson P. V. (1993). Letting go of outlived professional identities: A study of role and role strain for principals in restructured schools. *Educational Administration Quarterly, 29*(1), 34–68.

Buckingham, M. (1999). *First, break all the rules: What the world's greatest managers do differently.* New York: Simon and Schuster.

Burns, J. M. (1978). *Leadership.* New York: Harper and Row.

Church, A. H. (1997). Managerial self-awareness in high-performing individuals in organizations. *Journal of Applied Psychology, 82*(2), 281–292.

Collins, J. (2001). *Good to great.* New York: HarperCollins Publishers.

Derksen, J., Kramer, I., & Katzko M.(2002). Does a self report measure for emotional intelligence assess something different than general intelligence? *Personality and Individual Differences, 32*(1), 37–48.

Dufour, R. (2007). Professional learning communities: A bandwagon, an idea worth considering, or our best hope for high levels of learning? *Middle School Journal, 39*(1), 4–8.

Dufour, R., & Eaker, R. (1998). *Professional learning communities at work: Best practices for enhancing student achievement.* Bloomington, IN: National Educational Service.

Evans, R. (1996). *The human side of change.* San Francisco: Jossey-Bass.

Fletcher, C., & Baldry, C. (2003). Assessing self-awareness: Some issues and methods. *Journal of Managerial Psychology, 18*(5), 395–404.

Fullan, M. (2001). *Leading in a culture of change.* San Francisco: Jossey-Bass.

Garmston, R., & Wellman, B. (2009). *The adaptive school. A sourcebook for developing collaborative groups.* Norwood, MA: Christopher-Gordon.

Gardner, L., & Stough, C. (2002). Examining the relationship between leadership and emotional intelligence in senior level managers. *Leadership & Organization Development Journal, 23*(2), 68–78.

Geher, G., & Renstrom, K. L. (2004). Measurement issues in emotional intelligence research. In G. Geher (Ed.), *Measuring emotional intelligence: Common ground and controversy* (pp. 4–19). Hauppauge, NY: Nova Science Publishers.

Genos Emotional Intelligence Accreditation Manual. (2005). Swinburne University, Australia: Genos Pty Ltd.

George, J. M. (2000). Emotions and leadership: The role of emotional leadership. *Human Relations, 53*(8), 1027–1055.

Goleman, D. (1995). *Emotional intelligence.* New York: Bantam Books.

HayGroup. (1999). Findings from the *Fortune Magazine*/HayGroup 1999 Executive Survey of Leadership Effectiveness. *What makes great leaders? Rethinking the route to effective leadership.* Unpublished Report of The Hay Group, Boston.

Heifetz, R. A., & Linsky, M. (2002). *Leadership on the line: Staying alive through the dangers of leading.* Boston: Harvard Business School Press.

Higgs, M., & Aitken, P. (2003). An exploration of the relationship between emotional intelligence and leadership potential. *Journal of Managerial Psychology, 18*(8), 814–823.

Law, K. S., Song, L. J., & Wong, C. S. (2004). The construct and criterion validity of emotional intelligence and its potential utility for management studies. *Journal of Applied Psychology, 89*(3), 483–496.

Mandell, B., & Pherwani, S. (2003). Relationship between emotional intelligenceand transformational leadership style: A gender comparison. *Journal of Business and Psychology, 17*(3), 387–403.

Moore, B. L. (2007). *The emotional intelligence coaching of school administrators: A comparative case study.* Paper presented at the First International Congress on Emotional Intelligence, Malaga, Spain: September 19, 2007.

Palmer, B. (2003a). *An analysis of the relationships between various models and measures of emotional intelligence.* Unpublished doctoral dissertation. Swinburne University, Victoria, Australia.

Sala, F. (2001). *Do programs designed to increase emotional intelligence at work-work?* Unpublished Report of The Hay Group, Boston.

Sala, F. (2002). Leadership in education: Effective U.K. college principals. Unpublished Report of The Hay Group, Boston.

Salovey, P., & Mayer, J. D. (1990). Emotional intelligence. *Imagination, Cognition and Personality, 9*(3), 185–211.

Schlechty, P. C. (1997). *Inventing better schools: An action plan for educational reform.* San Francisco, CA: Jossey-Bass.

Senge, P. M. (1990). *The fifth discipline. The Art and practice of the learning organization.* New York: Doubleday.

Stone, H., Parker, J. D., & Wood, L. M. (2005). *Report on the Ontario Principals' Council Leadership Study.* Retrieved October 15, 2005, from Rutgers University, The Consortium for Research on Emotional Intelligence in Organizations Web site: http://www.eiconsortium.org/

Sy, T., Tram, S., & O'Hara (2006). Relation of employee and manger emotional intelligence to job satisfaction and performance. *Journal of Vocational Behavior, 68*(3), 461–473.

Van Rooy, D. L., & Viswesvaran, C. (2004). Emotional intelligence: A meta-analytic investigation of predictive validity and nomological net. *Journal of Vocational Behavior, 65*(1), 71–95.

Wheatley, M. J. (1999). *Leadership and the new science: Discovering order in a chaotic world.* San Francisco: Berrett-Koehler Publisher.

Williams, H. (2008). Characteristics that distinguish outstanding urban principals: Emotional intelligence, social intelligence and environmental adaptation. *Journal of Management Development, 27*(1), 36–54.

LaVergne, TN USA
05 March 2010

175067LV00001B/4/P